# Looking unto Jesus

# Looking unto Jesus

The Christ-Centered Piety of Seventeenth-Century Baptists

J. STEPHEN YUILLE

◆PICKWICK *Publications* • Eugene, Oregon

LOOKING UNTO JESUS
The Christ-Centered Piety of Seventeenth-Century Baptists

Copyright © 2013 J. Stephen Yuille. All rights reserved. Except for brief quotations in critical publications or reviews, no part of this book may be reproduced in any manner without prior written permission from the publisher. Write: Permissions, Wipf and Stock Publishers, 199 W. 8th Ave., Suite 3, Eugene, OR 97401.

Pickwick Publications
An Imprint of Wipf and Stock Publishers
199 W. 8th Ave., Suite 3
Eugene, OR 97401

www.wipfandstock.com

ISBN 13: 978-1-62032-177-5

*Cataloguing-in-Publication data:*

Yuille, J. Stephen.

   Looking unto Jesus : the Christ-centered piety of seventeenth-century Baptists / J. Stephen Yuille.

   xxiv + 96 pp. ; 23 cm. Includes bibliographical references.

   ISBN 13: 978-1-62032-177-5

   1. Spiritual life—History of doctrines—17th century. 2. Puritans—History—17th century. 3. Baptists—History—17th century. I. Title.

BX6231 Y85 2013

Manufactured in the U.S.A.

For my mom & dad

# Contents

*Foreword* by Tom. J. Nettles | ix

*Introduction* | xv

**1** A Guide to Eternal Glory *by Thomas Wilcox* | 1

**2** The Christ-Centered Piety of Thomas Wilcox | 16

**3** Saving Faith Discovered in Three Heavenly Conferences *by Vavasor Powell* | 39

**4** The Christ-Centered Piety of Vavasor Powell | 67

*Conclusion* | 91

*Bibliography* | 93

# Foreword

THOMAS CROSBY SET HIS hand to write a *History of the English Baptists* in 1738. An early pastor of his church, Benjamin Stinton, an "ingenious collector" of Baptist material, had submitted what he gathered to Crosby. Friends convinced Crosby to give the material to Daniel Neal that he might include the Baptists in his *The History of the Puritans*. On that matter Crosby commented, "under which general name, I did apprehend the English Baptists might very well be included."[1] Neal, however, in Crosby's opinion, dealt slightly and condescendingly to the Baptists and did not do either them or the material he possessed justice. Though both the strengths and weaknesses of Crosby's work are remarkable, none can doubt that he saw the Baptists as an integral part of that great movement of Puritanism, a more purely, primitive expression of it than those that adhered to that "pillar of popery," the baptism of infants.

The great strength of Puritanism, however, lay precisely in its implications for a disciplined church willing to suffer for truth and righteousness. Its weakness lay in its embracing of the chimera of a purified parish church integrally connected to the state church. The Great Ejection of 1662 renewed the Puritan opportunity to suffer and focus more precisely on issues of doctrine, spiritual experience, and assurance. Within this context the Baptists showed the points at which they most resembled the Puritans. That is one thing this book demonstrates with utter clarity.

Before the Great Ejection, fifty years earlier in fact, Thomas Helwys returned to England from a self-imposed exile in Amsterdam in order to provide a witness for the truth and against soul-destructive error to his "natural country men," many of whom were their "loving kindred in the

---

1. Crosby, *The History of the English Baptists*, 1:ii.

flesh," and others their "most worthy and dear friends to whom we owe the best fruits of our lives and the entire affection of our hearts."[2]

Helwys most useful and justly celebrated writing, *The Mistery of Iniquity*, denounced the state church system and issued a clear and unalloyed call for liberty of conscience. He included an uncompromised criticism of the "so much applauded profession of Puritanism" for clinging to the hope of a purified Anglicanism and a consequent inclusion in the establishment. Submission of conscience to Parliament was a spiritual atrocity in Helwys's view and of the essence of an anti-Christian posture. He challenged them with a keen observation about their agitation of Parliament for further reform of the state church.

> By this you testify against yourselves that you are unreformed, and that there is a way of reformation, of which you would be, if you might have leave or license to enter into it. Seeing you cannot obtain it, you justify that it is lawful to walk in an unreformed profession upon this ground because you may not have leave by act of Parliament to reform. What more false profession can be found on earth than this of yours, who profess that you know a way of much truth in which you would walk, but you do not, because you cannot by superior power be permitted.[3]

Helwys's commitment to liberty of conscience put him miles ahead of any other English thinker of the day. He contended that "none should be punished either with death or bonds for transgressing against the spiritual ordinances of the New Testament, and that such offences should be punished only with the spiritual sword and censures" and then only in local congregations.[4] In addition, Helwys wrote plainly and forcefully to the king, that, like Helwys himself, he was but "dust and ashes." He granted to him all legitimate power commanded by Scripture but did not allow any power over conscience. Helwys pled, politely but forcefully, that the king might remove the power of the earthly sword from the prelates of the English church and that he might not seek any power over the consciences of his subjects. Helwys put even the political fears of the day in a new perspective with a transcendent vision for liberty. Its scope must have been baffling to his contemporaries.

2. Helwys, *The Life and Writings*, 67.
3. Ibid., 220f.
4. Ibid., 160.

> We still pray our lord the king that we may be free from suspicion for having any thoughts of provoking evil against those of the Romish religion in regard of their profession, if they are true and faithful subjects to the king. For we do freely profess that our lord the king has no more power over their consciences than over ours, and that is none at all. For our lord the king is but an earthly king, and he has not authority as a king but in earthly causes. If the king's people are obedient and true subjects, obeying all human laws made by the king, our Lord the king can require no more. For men's religion to God is between God and themselves. The king will not answer for it. Neither may the king be judge between God and man. Let them be heretics, Turks, Jews, or whatsoever, it does not appertain to the earthly power to punish them in the least measure.[5]

Another Puritan whose consistency led him to a Baptist position was the man of irrepressible conscience, Roger Williams. Flourishing in his views thirty years later than Helwys, he pointed out, as did Helwys, the inconsistency of a Puritan's seeking the privilege of "parish" ministry. Only recently had Puritanism led to the insight that God's "people are a Company or Church of living stones," which made necessary separation from any concept of a parish church, that depended on a national church, that contained "the rubbish of Antichristian confusions and desolations."[6]

Questioning the attempts of Parliament in 1644 to establish Presbyterianism, Roger Williams employed a historical argument as a demonstration of the utter futility of seeking to establish true religion by governmental power. "Who knows not in how few years the Common weale of England hath set up and pull'd down: The Fathers made the children Hereticks, and the Children the Fathers. How doth the Parliament in Henry the VIII his days condemn the absolute Popery in Henry the VII? How is in Edwards the VI his time the Parlament [sic] of Henry the VIII condemned for their halfe popery halfe Protestantism? How soon dothe Queen Maries Parlament condemn Edward for his absolute Protestantisme? And Elizabeths Parlament as soon condemn Queen Maries for their absolute Popery?" Williams objected to the Parliament's efforts to seek a mold and pattern of church government from Holland or Scotland. They were on a path of oppression of "many thousand precious souls, for whom [Jesus] hath paid

---

5. Ibid., 209.

6. Roger Williams, "The Bloudy Tenent of Persecution" in *The Complete Writings of Roger Williams*, 3:66–67.

*Foreword*

so dear a ransome" and under the pretense of honoring him, they "oppose the Truth and Purity of his last will and Testament." He knew that the command of a king or the act of a parliament could be changed in a day, and certainly in a generation, so that neither truth nor peace were honored in the religious settlements imposed by rulers. "And, Oh!" he exclaimed as he considered the consequences of the effort to establish by law a particular denomination, "Since the common-weale cannot without a spirituall rape force the consciences of all to one Worship, oh that it may never commit that rape, in forcing the consciences of all men to one Worship, which a stronger arme and Sword may soon (as formerly) arise to alter."[7]

He made a very bold argument, showing that he had fully embraced the Baptist viewpoint on this issue and was ready to expand it to proportions far in advance of any of his contemporaries: "It is the will and command of God, that (since the coming of his Sonne the Lord Jesus) a permission of the most Paganish, Jewish, Turkish, or Antichristian consciences and worships, bee granted to *all* men in all Nations and Countries: and they are onely to bee fought against with that Sword which is only (in Soule matters) able to conquer, to wit, the Sword of God's Spirit, the Word of God."[8] Williams molded the symmetry and contours of his views of liberty of conscience as a Puritan seeking a purer application of the body of divinity commonly held.

The Puritans, however, continued their wonderfully experiential doctrinal writing and preaching as well as their futile attempts at establishing themselves as the Church of England sans the *Book of Common Prayer*. This all ended with the restoration of Charles II, the aggressiveness of a resolutely Anglican Parliament, and the iron-willed purpose of Lord Clarendon to squash all parties that refused to conform. In 1662 the Act of Uniformity, the second act of the Clarendon Code, ended from a political standpoint the Puritan movement. Baptists were now joined by the fellow [lower-case] puritan soul-physicians in the sanctifying pressures of oppression. In this fellowship of transcendent truth we find the Baptists Thomas Wilcox and Vavasor Powell. Stephen Yuille notes:

> In describing Thomas Wilcox and Vavasor Powell as Puritans, I am not referring to their political or ecclesiastical views, but their piety—what we might call "experimental Calvinism." The Puritans hold to the conviction that we must experience an affective

---

7. Williams, *Complete Writings*, 2:260.
8. Ibid., 3:3.

*Foreword*

appropriation of God's sovereign grace, moving beyond intellectual assent to heartfelt dedication to Christ. This piety transcends the divide that exists between those of differing political and ecclesiastical views: Independents and Presbyterians, Parliamentarians and Royalists, Conformists and Nonconformists.

Stephen Yuille sets a banqueting table for the reader both in the original texts he includes and in his own comments on these texts. The introduction he gives to the book on the appeal of Puritan divinity sets the table in a tantalizing way, and does not only tease with the promise of satisfaction but delivers the goods. His ability to bring to bear an impressive synthesis of Puritan authors on the subjects dealt with in these pages gives an intoxicating taste of the riches of Puritan divinity, particularly the doctrine of justification and the suitableness and aggressiveness of Christ as a savior of sinners. I believe that Stephen Yuille has delightfully accomplished his purpose in publishing: "to heighten your appreciation of Puritan (and early Baptist) piety and, above all else, point you to 'the unsearchable riches of Christ.'"

Dr. Tom. J. Nettles<br>
Professor of Historical Theology<br>
The Southern Baptist Theological Seminary

# Introduction

My first introduction to the Puritans was a seminary course—almost twelve years ago. The required reading included John Bunyan's *The Pilgrim's Progress*, Jonathan Edwards's *The Religious Affections*, and Richard Baxter's *The Reformed Pastor*. It was the closest I think I will ever come to an epiphany. I am exceedingly grateful, as it changed the course of my life—theologically, ecclesiastically, and spiritually. Since then, I have maintained a steady diet of Puritan writings. There are four reasons I keep coming back for more.

## GOD-FEARING

To begin with, the Puritans are God-fearing. That is to say, they believe in a great and glorious God. "If God be so great a God," writes George Swinnock, "how greatly is he to be reverenced! Canst thou do too much service for him, or give too much glory to him? Can thy love to him be too great, or can thy fear of him be too great . . . God is great, and therefore greatly to be feared."[9]

Years ago, my wife and I had the opportunity to visit Victoria Falls in Zimbabwe. On the spur of the moment, we decided to go kayaking. Our guide organized a breakfast for us on the banks of the Zambezi River. It was beautiful. He then provided a brief training session, followed by a stern warning: "This is a wild river. You'll have no problem with the crocodiles, as long as you remain in your kayak. But the hippos are another matter entirely. If they feel threatened by you, they'll strike from below!" He proceeded to snap a twig and announced (with what I think was a twinkle in his eye): "A hippo will vaporize your kayak!" I was ready to back out, but the peer-pressure was too great. And so we proceeded on our kayaking

---

9. Swinnock, *Works*, 3:330.

adventure. It was delightful until near the end of the trip when we entered a narrow stretch of the river. Suddenly, four sets of eyes appeared on the surface of the water.[10]

According to John Flavel, what I experienced at that moment is known as *natural* fear: "The trouble or perturbation of mind, from the comprehension of approaching evil or impending danger."[11] For Flavel, this is an essential part of human nature, meaning we fear what threatens us and, in response, we avoid what we fear. He proceeds to explain that there are two other kinds of fear: *holy* and *sinful*. Swinnock refers to these as *filial* and *servile*.[12] William Gurnall describes them as *holy* and *slavish*.[13] Stephen Charnock labels them *reverential* and *bondage*.[14] What are these Puritans talking about? Simply put, they are affirming that there are two ways to fear God: a *good* way and a *bad* way.

Their distinction is biblical. It is evident, for example, in Exodus 20. The Israelites are gathered at Sinai. They see the fire and smoke and hear the thunder. As a result, they are afraid. But Moses says to them, "*Fear not*: for God is come to prove you, and that *his fear* may be before your face, that ye sin not."[15] The distinction is also evident in 1 Samuel 12. The Israelites have sinned by requesting a human king. They see the rain and hear the thunder. As a result, they "greatly" fear God.[16] But Samuel says to them, "*Fear not*: Ye have done all this wickedness: yet turn not aside from following the LORD, but serve the LORD with all your heart."[17] A little later, he adds, "Only *fear* the LORD, and serve him in truth with all your heart: for consider how great things he hath done for you."[18] In short, both Moses and Samuel command the people not to fear God, yet to fear God. How do we explain this apparent contradiction? "Mark it," says John Bunyan, "here are two fears: a fear forbidden and a fear commended."[19]

---

10. The fact that I have written this should give some indication of how the incident turned out.

11. Flavel, *Works*, 3:245.

12. Swinnock, *Works*, 3:295.

13. Gurnall, *Christian in Complete Armour*, 1:119, 222, 263, 372, 373; 2:579.

14. Charnock, *Existence and Attributes of God*, 1:27, 41, 98, 172, 231, 236, 254; 2:107–9.

15. Exod 20:20. Italics mine. All Scripture quotations are from the Authorized Version.

16. 1 Sam 12:18.

17. 1 Sam 12:20. Italics mine.

18. 1 Sam 12:24. Italics mine.

19. Bunyan, *Fear of God*, 29.

*Introduction*

"Forbidden" fear, according to William Perkins, occurs "when a man only fears the punishment, and not the offence of God, or at least the punishment more than the offence."[20] In the above examples, the Israelites fear God, because they view him as a perceived threat. In other words, they regard him as hazardous to their well-being. This type of fear is merely concerned with self-preservation; hence, it falls short of making any lasting impression upon the soul. Gurnall explains, "Often we see God's judgments leave such an impression on men's spirits, that for a while they stand aloof from their sins . . . but when they see fair weather continue, and no clouds gather towards another storm, they descend to their old wicked practices, and grow more bold and heaven-daring than ever."[21] In a similar vein, Charnock remarks, "Many men perform those duties that the law requires with the same sentiments that slaves perform their drudgery; and are constrained in their duties by no other considerations but those of the whip and cudgel. Since, therefore, they do it with reluctance, and secretly murmur while they seem to obey, they would be willing that both the command were recalled, and the master that commands them were in another world."[22] Charnock goes on to argue that people actually desire the annihilation of what they fear will harm them. This means that ungodly fear is tantamount to desiring the annihilation of God.[23]

We find instances of such fear throughout Scripture. For example, in Moses' day, some of the Egyptian officials fear God. As a result, they bring their servants and cattle in from the field in order to avoid the devastation of the hailstorm.[24] However, it is an ungodly fear. They are only concerned with avoiding the perceived threat. They are only concerned with alleviating the danger. A little later, Moses says to Pharaoh, "But as for thee and thy servants, I know that ye will not yet fear the LORD God."[25] By way of another example, we read that the foreign inhabitants in the northern kingdom of Israel (transplanted by the king of Assyria after his invasion) fear God.[26] They view him as a source of potential harm, because he has sent lions among them to punish them for their idolatry. They commission one of the priests to instruct

---

20. Perkins, *Cases of Conscience*, 151.
21. Gurnall, *Christian in Complete Armour*, 1:289.
22. Charnock, *Existence and Attributes of God*, 1:98.
23. Ibid., 1:98–99.
24. Exod 9:20.
25. Exod 9:30.
26. 2 Kgs 17:25–41.

them in the worship of God. They go through the motions of worshipping him, while continuing to serve their own idols. In brief, they take steps to minimize the perceived threat to their well-being while remaining steadfast in their sin and rebellion. That is ungodly (forbidden) fear.

"Commended" fear, in marked contrast, does not arise from a perception of God as hazardous, but glorious. In other words, it flows from an appreciation of God.[27] According to William Gouge, godly fear "arises from faith in the mercy and goodness of God." When the soul feels "a sweet taste of God's goodness" and finds "that in his favour only all happiness consists, it is stricken with such an inward awe and reverence."[28] This sense of "awe and reverence" inclines the soul to do what pleases God, and to avoid what displeases him.[29] In simple terms, this means that "commended" fear (unlike "forbidden" fear) makes a divorce between sin and the soul.[30] It causes us to pursue holiness.[31] It compels us to surrender ourselves to God's will. In short, it results in "a careful endeavour to please God" and "a careful avoiding of such things as offend the majesty of God."[32]

This motif is front and center in the Puritan mindset. It is found in all their writings from William Perkins to Jonathan Edwards. They are acutely aware of the fact that they serve a great God—a God greatly to be feared. As Matthew Henry expresses it: "Of all things that are to be known this is most evident, that God is to be feared, to be reverenced, served, and worshipped; this is so the beginning of knowledge that those know nothing who do not know this."[33]

---

27. By way of example, see Gen 22:12; 42:18; Exod 3:6; 2 Sam 6:9; 1 Kgs 18:3; Neh 1:1; Job 1:1, 8–9; 2:2; Acts 9:31; 10:2, 22; Phil 2:12; Heb 11:7; and 1 Pet 1:17.

28. Gouge, *Domesticall Duties*, 8.

29. According to Flavel, godly fear "is a gracious habit or principle planted by God in the soul, whereby the soul is kept under a holy awe of the eye of God, and from thence is inclined to perform and do what pleases him, and to shun and avoid whatever he forbids and hates" (*Works*, 3:252).

30. By way of example, see Lev 19:14, 32; 25:17, 36, 43; Josh 24:14; 1 Sam 12:24; Pss 2:11; 112:1; Prov 14:2; Eccl 12:13; Acts 10:1–2, 35; Rom 11:20; Eph 5:21; Heb 4:1; 12:28–29; and Rev 19:5.

31. In this connection, Paul writes, "Having therefore these promises, dearly beloved, let us cleanse ourselves from all filthiness of the flesh and spirit, *perfecting holiness in the fear of God*" (2 Cor 7:1). Italics mine.

32. Gouge, *Domesticall Duties*, 8.

33. Henry, *Matthew Henry's Commentary*, 3:793.

## HEAVEN-SEEKING

In addition to God-fearing, the Puritans are heaven-seeking. As a boy, I remember hearing a preacher warn his congregation: "Some people are too heavenly-minded to be of any earthly good." At the time, that statement struck me as odd. Is it really possible to be too heavenly-minded? For the Puritans, the answer is an emphatic *no*! As a matter of fact, they affirm the exact opposite: "Some people are of no earthly good, because they are not heavenly-minded enough." Without heavenly-mindedness, we never persevere in the midst of affliction, never joyfully accept the loss of material possessions, never discipline ourselves for the purpose of godliness, and never strive to mortify sin. In a word, without heavenly-mindedness, we never grow spiritually.

But what exactly is it? For the Puritans, it is a spiritual foretaste of the joy that awaits us at glorification. Robert Bolton provides such a *foretaste* by encouraging his readers to consider "the place which God and all his blessed ones inhabit eternally,"[34] "the beauty and blessedness of glorified bodies,"[35] and "the unutterable happiness of the soul."[36] The apostle Paul confirms the validity of this approach, declaring, "For I reckon that the sufferings of this present time are not worthy to be compared with the glory which shall be revealed in us."[37] Here, he uses his power of reasoning to compare present "sufferings" and future "glory." What is his conclusion? Interestingly, he does not conclude that future glory is slightly greater than present suffering; nor does he conclude that future glory is twice as great as present suffering; nor does he conclude that future glory is one hundred or one thousand times greater than present suffering. He concludes that future glory so far outweighs present suffering that we cannot compare the two.

What is this glory? Paul explains, "For the earnest expectation of the creature waiteth for the manifestation of the sons of God."[38] "For we know," he adds, "that the whole creation groaneth and travaileth in pain together until now."[39] The groans associated with childbirth express present pain and (at the same time) a future expectation. It is the same for creation. Paul uses

---

34. Bolton, *Four Last Things*, 96.
35. Ibid., 105.
36. Ibid., 113.
37. Rom 8:18.
38. Rom 8:19. The expression "earnest expectation" literally means to watch with head outstretched.
39. Rom 8:22.

### Introduction

the imagery of childbirth, because creation's groans are anticipatory. One day, they will give birth to a new order—a new heaven and a new earth, in which righteousness dwells.[40] This new order is linked to "the manifestation of the sons of God." At that time, according to Flavel, we will be free from seven chains.[41] (1) We will be free from "defiling corruptions." The guilt of sin is pardoned by justification, and the power of sin is broken by sanctification, but the presence of sin is only removed at glorification. At that time, the lusts of the flesh and mind will be gone. We will enter a state of "perfect purity." (2) We will be free from "sinking sorrows." At present, because of affliction, we cry with Naomi: "Call me not Naomi [*pleasant*], call me Mara [*bitter*]."[42] But the day is coming when we will be free from all suffering. As the apostle John declares, "And God shall wipe away all tears from their eyes; and there shall be no more death, neither sorrow, nor crying, neither shall there be any more pain: for the former things are passed away."[43] In a word, we will enter a state of "fullness of joy." (3) We will be free from "entangling temptations." The devil is relentless in his assault "against our souls." However, in the future, "he can no more touch or affect the soul with any temptation, than we can batter the body of the sun with snow-balls." We will enter a state of "everlasting freedom." (4) We will be free from "distressing persecutions." "We must spend our days," says Flavel, "under the oppression of the wicked; yet this is our comfort, we know when we shall be far enough out of their reach." At that time, we will enter a state of "full and perfect rest." (5) We will be free from "pinching wants." We have temporal wants. More importantly, we have spiritual wants. We lack faith, joy, peace, love, and zeal. Plus, we struggle in spiritual duties. These deficiencies plague us. At glorification, however, every want will be supplied. We will enter a state of "universal supplies." (6) We will be free from "distracting fears." In that day, "no wind of fear shall ever ruffle or disturb their souls, and put them into a storm any more." We will enter a state of

---

40. Christ describes that event as the "regeneration" (Matt 19:28). Paul describes it as the gathering "together in one all things in Christ" and the reconciliation of "all things unto [Christ]" (Eph 1:10; Col 1:20). Peter describes it as "new heavens and a new earth, wherein dwelleth righteousness" (2 Pet 3:13). John describes it as "a new heaven and a new earth" (Rev 21:1). There is a beautiful description of that coming day in Isa 11:6–9. It culminates in these words: "For the earth shall be full of the knowledge of the LORD, as the waters cover the sea."

41. Flavel, *Works*, 3:113–17.

42. Ruth 1:20.

43. Rev 21:4.

*Introduction*

"highest security and rest." (7) We will be free from "deluding shadows." These are the deceitful vanities of the world. "Vanity of vanities, saith the Preacher; All is vanity."[44] These deluding shadows tempt us at present. One day, however, they will be but a shadow of a memory. And we will enter a state of "substantial good."

On that day, God will fully restore his image in us. Our minds will perceive him as the greatest good, and our hearts will love him as the greatest good. He will impress his glory upon us to the fullest capacity of our souls, and we will be satisfied. For the Puritans, contemplation of that day leads to a spiritual foretaste of the joy that awaits us. It is, for this reason, that they repeatedly emphasize the need for heavenly-mindedness. As Richard Baxter remarks, "I would not have you cast off your other meditations; but surely as heaven hath the pre-eminence in perfection, it should have it also in our meditation. That which will make us most happy when we possess it, will make us most joyful when we meditate upon it."[45]

## SIN-HATING

In addition to God-fearing and heaven-seeking, the Puritans are sin-hating. As a matter of fact, they go to great lengths to unmask sin's repugnancy. Why? They know we only mortify sin when we hate it. Prior to leaving for a trip to Ireland in 1999, I dutifully turned off the electricity in our apartment. However, I neglected to empty the fridge and freezer. We were living in Portugal at the time. It was July—the warmest month of the year. Two weeks later, we returned to our home, unaware of what was lurking behind the door. When I opened it, the smell of the putrefying meat was so strong that I nearly fell to my knees. It is precisely that sense of repugnancy that the Puritans seek to cultivate through their dark portrayal of sin.

For starters, they seek to convey sin's repugnancy by demonstrating its effect upon humanity. They go all the way back to Adam's sin, which resulted in his alienation from God. That deprivation had a negative impact upon Adam's faculties, meaning his will was no longer directed by an understanding that knew God or affections that desired God.[46] For the Puritans, that is the essence of original sin. Swinnock explains: "So hath original sin debauched

---

44. Eccl 12:8.
45. Baxter, *Practical Works*, 91.
46. See Eph 4:18–19.

the mind, and made it think crooked things straight, and straight things crooked; loathsome things lovely, and lovely things loathsome; perverted the will, and made it, as a diseased stomach, to call for and eat unwholesome meat against his own reason; enthralled his affections to sensuality and brutishness; chained the whole man, and delivered it up to the law of sin, and laid those strengths of reason and conscience in fetters, by which it might be hindered in its vicious inclinations and course of profaneness."[47] Here, Swinnock affirms that original sin has "debauched" the mind, "perverted" the will, and "enthralled" the affections. In essence, original sin has "chained the whole man." Bolton echoes this sentiment, stating, "My mind is blind, vain, foolish, my will perverse and rebellious, all my affections out of order, there is nothing whole or sound within me."[48] That has been the predicament of Adam's posterity ever since the fall. Because of the corruption of his nature, Adam could not transmit the perfect nature of his soul to his descendants. Instead, he transmitted the corrupt nature acquired by the fall. As a result, all of us are "dead in trespasses and sins."[49]

The Puritans also seek to convey sin's repugnancy by demonstrating its affront to God. They make it clear that at the root of all sin is the desire to substitute God with *self*. This necessarily means that sin is opposed to God's sufficiency. In the words of Jeremiah Burroughs: "As far as sin appears, it holds this forth before all and speaks this language: that there is not enough good in God, that is, the Blessed, Glorious, All-Sufficient, Eternal, Unchangeable Good and Fountain of all Good. Yet sin makes this profession, that there is not enough good in God to satisfy this soul, or else why does the soul depart from him in any sinful way and go to the creature for any good if there is enough in God himself?"[50]

Not only is sin opposed to God's sufficiency, but it is opposed to God's existence. For Ralph Venning, sin "makes the sinner wish and endeavour that there might be no God, for sinners are haters of God."[51] Swinnock agrees, "Sin is incomparably malignant, because the God principally injured by it is incomparably excellent."[52] It is "a breach of this incomparable God's law," "a contempt of this incomparable God's authority," "a dishonouring

---

47. Swinnock, *Works*, 2:166.
48. Bolton, *Carnal Professor*, 19.
49. Eph 2:1.
50. Burroughs, *Evil of Evils*, 58.
51. Venning, *Sinfulness of Sin*, 35.
52. Swinnock, *Works*, 4:456.

this incomparable God, whose name alone is excellent," and "a destroying this incomparable God."[53]

Due to their vivid portrayal of sin, the Puritans are often viewed as dark and dour killjoys. That is an unfortunate misrepresentation. Their description of the depths of our depravity is entirely biblical. Moreover, it is absolutely necessary as it arises from their firm conviction that we only mortify what we hate. A view of sin's repugnancy is the only thing that will produce the necessary impetus for mortification—the daily overthrowing of sin's dominion.

## CHRIST-EXALTING

The final reason why I am continually drawn to the Puritans is the fact that they are Christ-exalting.[54] In the opening verses of his epistle to the Ephesians, the apostle Paul tells us that we are "blessed" in Christ, "chosen" in Christ, "redeemed" in Christ, "predestined" in Christ, and "sealed" in Christ.[55] His point is that salvation from start to finish rests upon Christ. For the Puritans, there is nothing more soul-satisfying than contemplating Christ and our interest in him. In the words of John Owen, "Unto them that believe unto the saving of the soul, [Christ] is, he always hath been, precious—the sun, the rock, the life, the bread of their souls—everything that is good, useful, amiable, desirable, here or unto eternity."[56]

It is this soul-satisfying contemplation of Christ that I seek to expound in the present work: *Looking Unto Jesus*.[57] For assistance, I turn to two lesser-known Puritans: Thomas Wilcox and Vavasor Powell.[58] I have selected these

---

53. Ibid., 4:457–58.

54. They are not unique in this regard. For a brief synopsis of this emphasis in John Calvin, see Alexander, "The Supremacy of Jesus Christ," 109–18.

55. Eph 1:3–14.

56. Owen, *Works*, 1:3.

57. The title is taken from Heb 12:1–2, "Run with patience the race that is set before us, *looking unto Jesus* the author and finisher of faith; who for the joy that was set before him, endured the cross, despising the shame, and is set down at the right hand of the throne of God." Italics mine.

58. In describing Thomas Wilcox and Vavasor Powell as Puritans, I am not referring to their political or ecclesiastical views but their piety—what we might call "experimental Calvinism." The Puritans hold to the conviction that we must experience an affective appropriation of God's sovereign grace, moving beyond intellectual assent to heartfelt

*Introduction*

two—in part because of their anonymity—but more importantly because both are Baptists. Interestingly, seventeenth-century Baptist piety and Puritan piety intersect at numerous junctures. One of my goals is to demonstrate this interconnectedness as it pertains to their Christ-centered piety.

As for methodology, my approach is simple. Chapter 1 contains an edition of Thomas Wilcox's *A Guide to Eternal Glory*. Chapter 2 analyzes his Christ-centered piety, focusing on what he says about our need to apply Christ's blood, seek Christ's presence, prize Christ's righteousness, and esteem Christ's priesthood. Chapter 3 contains an edition of Vavasor Powell's *Saving Faith Discovered in Three Heavenly Conferences*. Chapter 4 analyzes his Christ-centered piety, focusing on his description of Christ as Shepherd, Judge, and Husband.

My prayer is that the Lord will use the following chapters to heighten your appreciation of Puritan (and early Baptist) piety and, above all else, point you to "the unsearchable riches of Christ."[59]

---

dedication to Christ. This piety transcends the divide that exists between those of differing political and ecclesiastical views: Independents and Presbyterians, Parliamentarians and Royalists, Conformists and Nonconformists. For more on this, see Yuille, *Puritan Spirituality*, 5–17.

59. Eph 3:8.

# 1

# A Guide to Eternal Glory[1]

## TO THE CHRISTIAN READER

Christian Reader, I find in this latter day the love of God shining in some measure, with its pleasant beams, in my heart, warming my affections, enflaming my soul, not only to give a spiritual echo in soul-duty to so great a lover as my Savior, whose transcendent love "passeth knowledge" (Eph. 3:19), but also to love and wish well to all Zion's heaven-born children. I find in this day many poor souls tossed to and fro, ready to be "carried about with every wind of doctrine, by the sleight of men, and cunning craftiness, whereby they lie in wait to deceive" (Eph. 4:14); and that there are so many foundations to build upon, which are false, upon which much labor is spent in vain; and that men are not speaking the truth in love, neither are they growing up "into him in all things, which is the head, even Christ" (Eph. 4:15). If there be a disjunction from Christ, there cannot be a growing in him; and without our union in him, all that we do is cursed.

You will find, therefore, Courteous Reader, this ensuing little treatise, if the Lord be pleased to bless the reading of it unto you, as a still voice behind you, saying, "This is the way, walk in it, that you turn not to the right hand or to the left." For the way into that pleasant path of soul-justification before God is in and through the righteousness of Jesus Christ; for all our

---

1. The full title is: *A Guide to Eternal Glory; or, Brief Directions to All Christians, How to Attain a True and Saving Interest in Christ, In Order to Their Everlasting Salvation.*

self-righteousness is as filthy rags, for "Surely, shall one say, in the LORD have I righteousness and strength . . . In the LORD shall all the seed of Israel be justified, and shall glory" (Isa. 45:24–25). It is only the dying of that just one, for us unjust ones, must bring us to God. He, who knew no sin, was made sin for us, that we (who were nothing but sin) "might be made the righteousness of God in him" (2 Cor. 5:21).

Christian Reader, let all that is of old Adam in you fall down at the foot of Christ. He only must have pre-eminence. All the vessels of this new spiritual, new covenant temple, from the cups to the flagons,[2] must be all hung upon Christ. He is to bear the glory, for he alone is worthy. He is to build the temple of the Lord, and to bear the glory. He, by his Father's appointment, is the foundation-stone, corner-stone, and is to be the top-stone. He is the Father's fullness of grace and glory. Whatever your wants be, you may come to him. There is balsam enough in him fit for soul-cure.

Reader, may the good Lord help you to experience this ensuing word of advice, that it may be made by God unto you, like honey, sweet to your soul and health to your bones; and my soul will rejoice with you.

Your brother in the faith and fellowship of the gospel,<br>Thomas Wilcox

## A GUIDE TO ETERNAL GLORY

A word of advice to my own heart and yours. You are a professor, and you partake of all ordinances; you do well. They are glorious ordinances. But if you have not the blood of Christ at the root of your profession, it will wither and prove but painted pageantry in which to go to hell. If you retain guilt or self-righteousness under it, those vipers will eat out all its vitals at length. Try and examine with the greatest strictness every day what bottom your profession and hope of glory is built upon, whether it was laid by the hand of Christ. If not, it will never be able to endure the storm that must come against it. Satan will throw it all down, and great will be the fall thereof (Matt. 7:27).

Glorious Professor! You will be winnowed. Every vein of your profession will be tried to purpose. It is terrible to have it all come tumbling down, and to find nothing but it to bottom upon.

---

2. I.e., pitchers.—ed.

Soaring Professor! See to your waxen wings, which will melt with the heat of temptations. What a misery, to trade much and break at length, having no stock, no foundation laid for eternity in your soul!

Gifted Professor! Look there be not a worm at the root that will spoil all your fine gourd, and make it die about you in a day of scorching.

Look over your soul daily, and ask, "Where is the blood of Christ to be seen upon my soul? What righteousness is it that I stand upon to be saved by? Have I got off all my self-righteousness?" Many eminent professors have come at length to cry out in the sight of the ruin of their duties, "Undone, undone to all eternity!"

The greatest sins can be hid under the greatest duties, and the greatest terrors. Make sure the wound that sin has made in your soul be perfectly cured by the blood of Christ, not skinned over with duties, humiliations, enlargements, etc. Apply what you will besides the blood of Christ, and it will poison the sore; you will find that sin was never truly mortified, and that you have not seen Christ bearing for you upon the cross. Nothing can kill sin but the beholding of Christ's righteousness.

Nature can afford no balsam fit for soul-cure. Healing from duty, and not from Christ, is the most desperate disease. Poor ragged nature, with all its highest improvements, can never spin a garment fine enough (without spot) or large enough (without patches) to cover the soul's nakedness. Nothing can fit the soul for that use but Christ's perfect righteousness.

Whatever is of nature's spinning must be all unraveled before the righteousness of Christ can be put on. Whatever is of nature's putting on, Satan will come and plunder every rag of it away, and leave the soul naked and open to the wrath of God. All that nature can do will never make up the least dram[3] of grace, which can mortify sin or look Christ in the face one day.

You are a professor, you go to hearing, praying, and receiving, yet miserable might you be. Look about you; did you ever yet see Christ to this day in distinction from all other excellencies and righteousness in the world, and all of them falling before the majesty of his love and grace (Isa. 2:17)?

If you have seen Christ truly, you have seen pure grace, pure righteousness in him, every way infinite, far exceeding all sin and misery. If you have seen Christ, you can trample upon all the righteousness of men and angels, so as to bring you into acceptance with God. If you have seen Christ, you would not do a duty without him for ten thousand worlds (1 Cor. 2:2). If ever you did see Christ, you saw him a Rock, higher than

---

3. I.e., a small unit of measurement.—ed.

self-righteousness, Satan, sin (Ps. 61:2), and the Rock does follow you (1 Cor. 10:4), and there will be continual droppings of honey and grace out of that Rock to satisfy you (Ps. 81:16).

Examine, if ever you did behold Christ as the only begotten of the Father, full of grace and truth (John 1:14–17). Be sure you have come to Christ, have stood upon the Rock of Ages, have answered his call to your soul, and have closed with him for justification.

Men talk bravely of believing, while whole and sound; but few know it. Christ is the mystery of the Scripture. Grace is the mystery of Christ. Believing is the most wonderful thing in the world. Put anything of your own to it, and you spoil it. Christ will not so much as look at it for believing.

When you believe and come to Christ, you must leave behind you your own righteousness, and bring nothing but your sin. Oh, that is hard! Leave behind all your holiness, sanctification, duties, humiliations, etc., and bring nothing but your wants and misery, or else Christ is not fit for you, nor you for Christ. Christ will be a pure Redeemer and Mediator, and you must be an undone sinner, or else Christ and you will never agree. It is the hardest thing in the world to take Christ alone for righteousness; that is, to acknowledge him Christ. Join anything to him of your own, and you un-Christ him.

Whatever comes in when you go to God for acceptance (besides Christ), call it Antichrist, bid it be gone, and make only Christ's righteousness triumphant. All besides that must fall, if Christ stand; and you will rejoice in the day of the fall thereof (Isa. 1:10–12). Christ alone did tread the wine-press, and there was none with him (Isa. 63:3). If you join to anything but Christ, Christ will trample upon it in fury and anger, and stain his raiment with the blood thereof.

You think it easy to believe. Was your faith ever tried with an hour of temptation and with a thorough sight of sin? Was it ever put to grapple with Satan and the wrath of God, lying upon the conscience? When you were in the mouth of hell and the grave, did God then show you Christ—a ransom, a righteousness, etc.? Could you then say, "Oh, I see grace enough in Christ?" If so, you may say that which is the biggest word in the world, "You believe." Untried faith is uncertain faith.

To believing there must go a clear conviction of sin, and of the merits of the blood of Christ, and of Christ's willingness to save upon this consideration merely, that you are a sinner; things all harder than to make a world. All the power in nature cannot get up so high in a storm of sin and guilt, as really to believe there is any grace, any willingness in Christ to save.

When Satan charges sin upon the conscience, then for the soul to charge it upon Christ, that is gospel-like, that is to make him Christ. He serves for that use. To accept Christ's righteousness alone, his blood alone for salvation, that is the sum of the gospel. When the soul in all duties and distresses can say, "Nothing but Christ, Christ alone, for righteousness, justification, sanctification, and redemption (1 Cor. 1:30), not humiliations, not duties, not graces, etc.," that soul has got above the reach of the billows.[4]

All temptations, Satan's advantages, and our complaints, are laid in self-righteousness and self-excellency. God pursues these by setting Satan upon you (as Laban did Jacob for his images, which Rachel hid (Gen. 31:30)). These must be torn from you (be as unwilling as you might be). These hinder Christ from coming in. Until Christ comes in, guilt will not go out; and where guilt is, there is hardness of heart. Therefore, much guilt argues little (if anything) of Christ. When guilt is raised up, take heed of getting it allayed any way but by Christ's blood; anything else will tend to hardening. Make Christ your peace (Eph. 2:14), not your duties, your tears, etc.; make Christ your righteousness, not your graces, etc. You will destroy Christ by resting in duties, as well as by sins. Look at Christ, and do as much as you will. Stand with all your weight upon Christ's righteousness. Take heed of having one foot on your own righteousness, and another on Christ's.

Until Christ comes and sits on high upon a throne of grace in the conscience, there is nothing but guilt, terrors, secret suspicions, the soul hanging between hope and fear, which is an ungospel-like state. He who fears to see sin's utmost violence, the utmost hell of his own heart, suspects the merits of Christ. Be you ever such a great sinner (1 John 2:1), try Christ to make him your Advocate, and you will find him Jesus Christ the righteous.

In all doubts, fears, and storms of conscience, look at Christ continually. Do not argue with Satan; he desires no better. Bid him go to Christ, and he will answer him. It is his office, as he is our Advocate (1 John 2:1). It is his office to answer law, as our Surety (Heb. 7:22). It is his office to answer justice, as our Mediator (Gal. 3:20; 1 Tim. 2:5). And he is sworn to that office (Heb. 7:20–21). Put Christ upon it. If you will do anything yourself as to satisfaction for sin, you renounce Christ the righteous, who was made sin for you (2 Cor. 5:21). Satan may allege[5] and corrupt Scripture, but he cannot answer Scripture. It is Christ's word of mighty authority. Christ foiled Satan with it (Matt. 4:1–11). In all the Scripture, there is not an ill

---

4. I.e., clouds.—ed.
5. I.e., quote.—ed.

## Looking unto Jesus

word against a poor sinner, stripped of self-righteousness; nay, it plainly points out this man to be the subject of the grace of the gospel, and none else. Believe but Christ's willingness, and that will make you willing.

If you find you cannot believe, remember it is Christ's work to make you believe. Put him upon it; he works "to will and to do of his good pleasure" (Phil. 2:13). Mourn for your unbelief, which is setting up of guilt in the conscience above Christ, undervaluing the merits of Christ, accounting his blood an unholy, a common, and an unsatisfying thing.

You complain much of yourself. Does your sin make you look more at Christ, less at self? That is right, else complaining is but hypocrisy. To be looking at duties, graces, enlargements, when you should be looking at Christ, that is pitiful. Looking at them will but make you proud. Looking at Christ's grace will make you humble. "By grace ye are saved" (Eph. 2:5).

In all your temptations be not discouraged (Jas. 1:2). Those surges may be, not to break you, but to have you off yourself, on to the Rock Christ. You may be brought low, even to the brink of hell, ready to tumble in, you cannot be brought lower than the belly of hell (many saints have been there), yet there you may cry, there you may look toward the holy temple (Jonah 2:2, 4). Into that temple, none can enter but purified ones, and with an offering too (Acts 21:26). But now Christ is our temple, sacrifice, altar, high-priest, to whom none must come but sinners, and that without any offering but his own blood, once offered (Heb. 7:27). Remember all the patterns of grace that are in heaven. You think, "Oh, what a monument of grace would I be!" There are many thousands of monuments as rich as you would be.

The greatest sinner did never pose[6] the grace of Christ. Do not despair; hope still. When the cloud is blackest, even then look towards Christ, the standing pillar of the Father's love and grace, set up in heaven for all sinners to gaze upon continually. Whatever Satan or conscience say, do not conclude against yourself. Christ will have the last word. He is judge of the quick and dead, and must pronounce the final sentence. His blood speaks reconciliation (Col. 1:20), cleansing (1 John 1:7), purchase (Acts 20:28), redemption (1 Pet. 1:19), purging (Heb. 9:13–14), remission (Heb. 5:22), liberty (Heb. 10:19), justification (Rom. 5:9), nearness to God (Eph. 2:13). Not a drop of his blood will be lost. Stand, and hearken to what God will say, for he will speak peace to his people, that they return no more to folly (Ps. 85:8). He speaks grace, mercy, and peace (2 Tim. 1:2). That is the language of the Father, and of Christ. Wait for Christ's appearing as the

---

6. I.e., challenge.—ed.

morning-star (Rev. 22:16). He will come as certainly as the morning, as refreshingly as the rain (Hos. 6:3). The sun may as well be hindered from rising as Christ, the Sun of righteousness (Mal. 4:2). Look not a moment off Christ. Look not upon sin, but look upon Christ first. When you mourn for sin, if you do not see Christ, then away with it (Zech. 12:10).

In every duty, look at Christ; before duty to pardon, in duty to assist, and after duty to accept. Without this, it is but carnal, careless duty. Do not legalize the gospel, as if part remained for you to do and suffer, and Christ were but a half-Mediator, and you must bear part of your own sin, and make part satisfaction. Let sin break your heart, but not your hope in the gospel.

Look more at justification than sanctification. In the highest commands, consider Christ, not as an exactor to require, but a debtor, an undertaker, to work. If you have looked at workings, duties, qualifications, etc. more than at the merits of Christ, it will cost you dear. No wonder you go complaining. Graces may be evidences, but only the merits of Christ must be the foundation for your hope to bottom on. Christ only can be "the hope of glory" (Col. 1:27).

When we come to God, we must bring nothing but Christ with us. Any ingredients of our own qualifications will poison and corrupt faith. He who builds upon duties, graces, etc. knows not the merits of Christ. This makes believing so hard, so far above nature. If you believe, you must every day renounce (as dung and dross (Phil. 3:7-8)) your privileges, your obedience, your sanctification, your duties, your graces, your tears, your meltings, your humiliations, and nothing but Christ must be held up. Every day, your workings, your self-sufficiency must be destroyed. You must take all out of God's hand. Christ is the gift of God (John 4:10). Faith is the gift of God (Eph. 2:8). Pardon is a free gift (Rom. 5:16). Ah, how nature storms, frets, and rages at this; that all is of gift, and it can purchase nothing with its own actions, and tears, and duties; that all its works are excluded, and of no value in heaven!

If nature had been responsible to contrive the way of salvation, it would have put it into any hands of saints or angels, to sell it, rather than into the hands of Christ, who gives freely, whom therefore it suspects. It would have set up a way to purchase by doing. Therefore, it abominates the merits of Christ, as a destructive thing to it. It would do anything to be saved, rather than go to Christ, or close with Christ. Christ will have nothing, but the soul will force something of its own upon Christ. Here is the great controversy.

Consider, did you ever yet see the merits of Christ, and the infinite satisfaction made by his death? Did you see this in a time when the burden of sin and the wrath of God lay heavy upon your conscience? That is grace. The greatness of Christ's merits is not known but to a poor soul at the greatest loss. Slight convictions will have but slight, low prizing of Christ's blood and merits.

Despairing Sinner! You are looking on your right hand and your left, saying, "Who will show us any good?" You are tumbling over all your duties and professions, to patch up a righteousness to save you. Miserable comforters are all those to you! Look at Christ now; look to him and be saved, all the ends of the earth (Isa. 45:22). There is none else. He is a Savior, and there is none besides him (Isa. 45:21). Look anywhere else, and you are undone.

God will look at nothing but Christ, and you must look at nothing else. Christ is lifted up on high (as the brazen serpent was in the wilderness), that the ends of the earth, sinners at the greatest distance, might see him, and look towards him.[7] The least sight of him will be saving, the least touch will be healing to you, and God intends you should look on him, for he has set him upon a high throne of glory in the open view of all poor sinners. You have infinite reason to look on him, no reason at all to look off him; for "he is meek and lowly in heart" (Matt. 11:29). He will do that himself which he requires of his creature, bear with infirmities (Rom. 15:1), not pleasing himself, not standing upon points of law (Rom. 15:2). He will restore with the spirit of meekness (Gal. 6:1), and bear your burdens (Gal. 6:2). He will forgive, not only until seven times, but seventy times seven (Matt. 18:21–22). It put the faith of the apostles to it to believe this (Luke 17:4–5). Because we are hard to forgive, we think Christ is hard.

We see sin great; we think Christ does too. We measure infinite love with our line, infinite merits with our sins, which is the greatest pride and blasphemy (Ps. 103:11–12; Isa. 40:15). Hear what he says, "I have found a ransom" (Job 33:24). "In him I am well pleased" (Matt. 3:17). God will have nothing else; nothing else will do you good, or satisfy conscience, but Christ, who satisfied the Father. God does all upon the account of Christ.

Your desserts are hell, wrath, and rejection; Christ's desserts are life, pardon, and acceptance. He will only show you the one, but he will give you the other. It is Christ's own glory and happiness to pardon. Consider, while Christ was upon the earth, he was more among publicans and sinners than Scribes and Pharisees (his professed adversaries), for they were righteous

---

7. See John 3:14–15.

ones. It is not as you imagine; that his state in glory makes him neglectful, scornful to poor sinners. No, he has the same heart now in heaven. He is God and changes not. He is "the Lamb of God, which taketh away the sin of the world" (John 1:29). He has gone through all your temptations, dejections, sorrows, desertions, rejections (Matt. 4:3–12; 26:38; Mark 15:34; Luke 22:44). He has drunk the bitterness of the cup, and left you the sweet; the condemnation is out. Christ drank up all the Father's wrath at one draught, and nothing but salvation is left for you.

You say that you cannot believe and cannot repent. You are fitter for Christ, if you have nothing but sin and misery. Go to Christ with all your impenitency, and unbelief, to get faith and repentance from him. That is glorious. Tell Christ, "Lord, I have brought no righteousness, no grace to be accepted in, or justified by; I am come for yours, and must have it." We would be bringing to Christ, and that must not be; not a penny of nature's highest improvements will pass in heaven. Grace will not stand with works (Rom. 11:6; Titus 3:5). That is a terrible point to nature, which cannot think of being stripped of all, not having a rag of duty or righteousness left to look at. Self-righteousness and self-sufficiency are the darlings of nature, which she preserves as her life. That makes Christ's righteousness such a strange thing to nature. She cannot desire him. He is just directly opposite to all nature's glorious interest. Let nature but make a gospel, and it would be quite contrary to Christ's. It would be for the just, the innocent, the holy, the righteous, etc. Christ has made the gospel for you; that is, for needy sinners, the ungodly, unrighteous, the unjust, the accursed. Nature cannot endure to think the gospel is only for sinners. It will rather choose to despair than go to Christ upon such terrible terms.

When nature is but put to it by guilt or wrath, it will go to its old haunts of self-righteousness, self-goodness, etc. An infinite power must cast down those strongholds. None but the self-justified stands excluded out of the gospel. Christ will look at the most abominable sinner before him, because to such a one Christ cannot be made justification, since he is no sinner. To say in compliment, "I am a sinner," is easy; but to pray with the publican indeed, "Lord, be merciful to me a sinner,"[8] is the hardest prayer in the world. It is easy to say, "I believe in Christ," but to see Christ full of grace and truth, of whose fullness you may receive grace for grace, is hard. It is easy to profess Christ with the mouth, but to confess him with the heart,

---

8. See Luke 18:13.

as Peter (to be the Christ, the Son of the living God, the only Mediator),[9] is above flesh and blood.

Many call Christ "Savior," but few know him so. To see grace and salvation in Christ is the greatest sight in the world. None can do that, but at the same time they will see that grace and salvation are theirs. Sights will cause applications. I may be ashamed to think that in the midst of so much profession, yet I have known little of the blood of Christ, which is the main thing of the gospel. A Christ-less, formal profession is the blackest sight, that can be, next to hell. You might have many good things, and yet let one thing be wanting, and it will make you go away sorrowful from Christ.

You have never sold all you have, never parted with all your own righteousness, etc.[10] You might be high in duty, and yet a perfect enemy and adversary to Christ. In every prayer, in every ordinance, labor after sanctification to your utmost, but make not a Christ of it to save you. If so, it must come down one way or other. Christ's infinite satisfaction, not your sanctification, must be your justification before God. When the Lord will appear terrible out of holy places, fire will consume all that as hay and stubble.

This will be found religion only, to bottom all upon the everlasting mountains of God's love and grace in Christ, to live continually in the sight of Christ's infinite righteousness and merits (they are sanctifying; without them, the heart is carnal); and in those sights to see the full vileness, yet littleness of sin, and to see all pardoned; and in those sights to pray, hear, etc., seeing your polluted self, and all your weak performances accepted continually; and in those sights to trample upon all your self-glories, righteousness, and privileges, as abominable, and to be found continually in the righteousness of Christ alone, rejoicing in the ruins of all your own righteousness, the spoiling of all your own excellencies, that Christ alone, as Mediator, may be exalted in his throne, mourning over all your duties (however glorious) that you have not performed in that sight and sense of Christ's love. Without the blood of Christ on the conscience, all is dead services (Heb. 9:14).

Christ is every way too magnificent a person for poor nature to close withal or apprehend. Christ is so infinitely holy that nature durst never look at him; so infinitely good that nature can never believe him to be such, when it lies under the full sights of sin. Christ is too high and glorious for nature so much as to touch. There must be a divine nature first put into the soul to make it lay hold on him. He lies so infinitely beyond the sight or

---

9. See Matt 16:16.
10. See Mark 10:17–22.

reach of nature. That Christ, that natural freewill can apprehend, is but a natural Christ of a man's own making. He is not the Father's Christ, not Jesus, the Son of the living God, to whom none can come without the Father's drawing (John 6:44, 46).

Finally, search the Scriptures daily, as mines of gold, wherein the heart of Christ is laid. Watch against constitution sins; see them in their vileness, and they will never break out into act. Keep always a humble, empty, broken frame of heart, sensible of any spiritual miscarriage, observant of all inward workings, fit for the highest communications. Keep not guilt in the conscience, but apply the blood of Christ immediately. God charges sin and guilt upon you, to make you look to Christ the brazen serpent.

Judge not Christ's love by providences, but by promises. Bless God for shaking you off your false foundations, for any way whereby he keeps the soul awakened, and looking after Christ. It is better to have sickness and temptations than security and slightness. A slight spirit will turn into a profane spirit, and will sin and pray too. Slightness is the ban of profession. If it be not rooted out of the heart by constant and serious dealings with and beholdings of Christ in duties, it will grow stronger and more deadly by being under church ordinances. Measure not your graces by others' attainments, but by Scripture trials. Be serious, exact in duty, having the weight of it upon the heart; but be as much afraid of taking comfort from duties, as of sins. Comfort from any hand but Christ's is deadly. Be much in prayer, or else you will never keep up much communion with God. As you are in closet-prayer, so you will be in all other ordinances.

Reckon not duties by high expressions, but by low frames and the beholdings of Christ. Tremble at duties and gifts. It was the saying of a saint, "He was more afraid of duties than his sins." The one often made him proud, the other always made him humble. Treasure up manifestations; they make the heart low for Christ, and too high for sin. Slight not the lowest, meanest evidence of grace. God may put you to make use of the lowest, as you think (1 John 3:14); even that may be worth a thousand worlds to you.

Be true to truth, but not turbulent and scornful. Restore such as are fallen; help them up again with all the bowels of Christ. Set the broken, disjointed bones with the grace of the gospel.

High Professor! Despise not weak saints. You might come to wish to be in the condition of the meanest of them. Be faithful to others' infirmities, but sensible of your own. Visit sick-beds and deserted souls often; they are excellent schools of experience. Abide in your calling. Be dutiful to all religions[11] as to the Lord. Be content with little of the world; little will serve. Think every little of earth too much, because unworthy of the least. Think much of heaven too little, because Christ is so rich and free. Think every one better than yourself, and carry every self-loathing about you, as one fit to be trampled upon by all the saints.

See the vanity of the world, and the consumption that is upon all things, and love nothing but Christ. Mourn to see so little of Christ in the world, so few needing him. Trifles please them better. To a secure soul, Christ is but a fable, and the Scriptures but a story. Mourn to think how many, under high professions, are not under grace, looking much after duty, little after Christ, little versed in grace. Prepare for the cross; welcome it; bear it triumphantly like Christ's cross, whether scoffs, mockings, jeers, contempts, imprisonments, etc. But see it be Christ's cross, not your own.

Sins will hinder from glorying in the cross of Christ. Omitting little truths against light will breed hell in the conscience, as well as committing the greatest sins against light. If you have been taken out of the belly of hell into Christ's bosom, and made to sit among princes in the household of God, oh, how you should live as a pattern of mercy! Redeemed, restored soul, what infinite sums do you owe Christ? With what singular frames must you walk, and do every duty? Sabbaths, what praising days, and singings of hallelujahs, should they be to you? Ordinances, what a heaven, a being with Christ, and angels, and saints? Baptism, what a drowning the soul in eternal love, as a burial with Christ, dying to all things beside him? Every time you think of Christ, be astonished and wonder! When you see sin, look at Christ's grace that pardoned it. When you are proud, look at Christ's grace. It will humble and strike you down in the dust.

Remember Christ's time of love, when you were naked (Ezek. 16:8–9), and he chose you. Can you ever have a proud thought? Remember whose arms supported you from sinking, and delivered you from the lowest hell (Ps. 86:13). Shout in the ears of angels and men (Ps. 14:8),[12] and sing forever, "Praise, grace, grace!" Daily, repent, and believe, and pray, and walk in the sights of grace, as one who has the anointings of grace upon you. Remember your sins, Christ's pardonings; your desserts, Christ's merits; your weakness, Christ's strength; your pride, Christ's humility; your many infirmities, Christ's restorings; your guilt, Christ's new application of his blood; your fallings, Christ's raising up; your slightness, Christ's sufferings;

11. Relations?—ed.
12. Ps 14:8 does not exist.—ed.

your want, Christ's fullness; your temptations, Christ's tenderness; your vileness, Christ's righteousness.

Blessed Soul, whom Christ will find not having on his own righteousness (Phil. 3:9), but having his robes washed and made white in the blood of the Lamb (Rev. 7:14). Woeful, Miserable Professor, who has not the gospel within! Rest not in church-trial; you might pass that, and be cast away in Christ's day of trial. You might come to baptism, and never come to Jesus and the blood of sprinkling (Heb. 12:24). Whatever workings or attainments come not up to clear, distinct apprehensions of Christ's blood, merits, and righteousness (the main object of the gospel), fall short of the gospel, and leaves the soul in a condition of doubtings and questionings. Doubtings, if not looked unto, will turn to a slightness of spirit, one of the most dangerous frames. Trifle not with ordinances. Be much in meditation and prayer. Wait diligently upon all hearing opportunities. We have need of doctrine, reproof, exhortation, consolation, as the tender herbs and grass have of the rain, the dew, the small rain, and the showers (Deut. 32:2). Do all you do as soul-work, as unto Christ (Zech. 7:5–6), as immediately dealing with Christ Jesus, as if he were looking on you, and you on him; and fetch all your strength from him.

Observe what holy motions you find in your soul to duties; prize the least motion that is from a sight of Christ, the least good thought you have of Christ, the least good word you speak of him sincerely from the heart, is rich mercy. Oh, bless God for it! Observe, every day, that you have the day-spring from on high (with his morning dews of mourning for sin) constantly visiting (Luke 1:17), the bright morning-star (with fresh influences of grace and peace) constantly arising (Rev. 22:16), and Christ sweetly greeting the soul in all duties. Whatever duty makes not more spiritual will make more carnal. Whatever does not quicken and humble will deaden and harden.

Judas might have the sop, the outward privilege of baptism, the Lord's Supper, church fellowship, etc., but John leaned on Christ's bosom (John 13:23). That is the gospel-ordinance posture, in which we should pray, and hear, and perform all duties. Nothing, but lying in that bosom, will dissolve hardness of heart, make you to mourn kindly for sin, and cure slightness and ordinariness of spirit (the gangrene in profession). That will humble indeed, and make the soul cordial to Christ, and sin vile to the soul; yea, it will transform the ugliest piece of hell into the glory of Christ.

Never think you are right as you should be, a Christian of any glorious attainment, until you come to this. Always see and feel yourself lying in the bosom of Christ, who is in the bosom of the Father (John 1:18). Come and move the Father for sights of Christ, and you will be sure to speed. You can come with no request that pleases him better. He gave him out of his own bosom for that very end, to be held up before the eyes of all sinners, as the everlasting monument of his Father's love.

Looking at the natural sun weakens the eye. The more you look at Christ, the Sun of righteousness, the stronger and clearer will the eye of faith be. Look but at Christ, and you will love him and live on him. Think on him continually. Keep the eye constantly upon Christ's blood, or else every blast of temptation will shake you. If you would see sin's sinfulness, to hate it, and mourn, do not stand looking upon sin, but look upon Christ first as suffering and satisfying.

If you would see your graces, your sanctification, do not stand gazing upon them, but look at Christ's righteousness in the first place. If you see the Sun, you see all. Then, look at your grace in the second place.

When you act faith, what you first look at, that you expect settlement from, and make it the bottom of your hope. Go to Christ in sight of your sin and misery, not of your grace and holiness. Have nothing to do with your graces and sanctification (they will but veil Christ) until you have seen Christ first. He who looks upon Christ through his graces is like one who sees the sun in water, which wavers and moves as the water does. Look upon Christ only, as shining in the firmament of the Father's love and grace. You will not see him but in his own glory, which is unspeakable.

Pride and unbelief will put you upon seeing somewhat in yourself first; but faith will have to do with none but Christ, who is inexpressibly glorious, and must swallow up your sanctification, as well as your sins. God made him both for us, and we must make him both (1 Cor. 1:30; 2 Cor. 5:21). He who sets up his sanctification to look at to comfort him sets up the greatest idol which will strengthen his doubts and fears. Do but look off Christ, and presently (like Peter) you sink in doubts.

A Christian never wants comfort, but by breaking the order and method of the gospel, looking on his own, and looking off Christ's perfect righteousness, which is to choose to live rather by candle-light than by the light of the Sun.

The honey that you suck from your own righteousness will turn into perfect gall; and the light you take from it, to walk in, will turn into black night upon the soul. Satan is tempting you, by putting you to plod about your own graces, to get comfort from them. Then, the Father comes and points you to Christ's grace (as rich and glorious, infinitely pleasing him), and bids you study Christ's righteousness (and his biddings and enablings). That is a blessed motion, a sweet whispering, checking your unbelief. Follow the least hint, close with much prayer, prize it as an invaluable jewel. It is an earnest of more to come again.

If you would pray and cannot, and so you are discouraged, see Christ praying for you, using his interest with the Father for you. What can you want (John 14:16; 17:1–20)? If you be troubled, see Christ your peace (Eph. 2:14), leaving you peace, when he went up to heaven, again and again charging you not to be troubled, no not in the least (sinfully troubled), so as to obstruct your comfort or your believing (John 14:1, 27). He is now upon the throne, having spoiled upon his cross (in the lowest state of his humiliation) all whatsoever can hurt or annoy you. He has borne all your sins, sorrows, fears, disgraces, sicknesses, troubles, temptations, and is gone to prepare mansions for you.

You, who has seen Christ all, and yourself absolutely nothing, who makes Christ all your life, and are dead to all righteousness besides, you are the Christian, one highly beloved, and who has found favor with God. Favorite of heaven, do Christ this one favor for all his love to you: love all his poor saints and children (the meanest, the weakest, notwithstanding any difference in judgment). They are engraved on his heart, as the names of the children of Israel on Aaron's breast-plate (Ex. 28:21). Let them be likewise on yours. Pray for the peace of Jerusalem; they will prosper that love her (Ps. 122:6).

# 2

# The Christ-Centered Piety of Thomas Wilcox[1]

IN *THE HISTORY OF the English Baptists*, Thomas Crosby provides the following description of Thomas Wilcox:

> Mr. Thomas Wilcox, elder of a small congregation, which met before the sickness, at his house on Cannon-street, afterwards, at the Three-cranes, in the Borough of Southwark.[2] He was two or three times put into Newgate for nonconformity, and suffered very much. He wrote a small piece, which was printed before the fire of London,[3] entitled, *A drop of honey from the rock Christ*. A piece that was very well esteemed, and has done much good, and been oft reprinted. He was born in the month of August 1622, at Linden, in the county of Rutland,[4] and died May 17th, 1687, in the 64th year of his age. He was a moderate man, and of catholic principles, well beloved by all denominations, and frequently preached among the Presbyterians and Independents. He left a widow and three children.[5]

---

1. Much of this chapter's content was originally presented as a paper at the annual conference of the Andrew Fuller Center (Southern Baptist Theological Seminary, Louisville, KY), August 2008.

2. The Borough of Southwark is located immediately south of London Bridge.

3. This is most likely a reference to the "great fire" in September 1666.

4. The County of Rutland is located in central England.

5. Crosby, *History of the English Baptists*, 3:101. There is another (far more famous)

## The Christ-Centered Piety of Thomas Wilcox

The above description of Thomas Wilcox leaves many questions unanswered. What was his family life like? Was he a good husband and father? What was his pastorate like? Was he a faithful elder? How did he survive the great fire of London? How did he manage during his imprisonments at Newgate? He was Baptist. How did he come to embrace his convictions? He was a contemporary of the likes of John Bunyan, John Owen, and Thomas Goodwin. Did he know any of these towering Puritans? By the time he celebrated his twentieth birthday, the Long Parliament was convened,[6] the Westminster Assembly was gathered, William Laud was imprisoned, the Court of High Commission was abolished,[7] the Civil War was underway, and the Solemn League and Covenant was signed. To put it simply, he lived through one of the most pivotal periods in the history of Great Britain. What did he make of it all? What were his political views? What did he think of Oliver Cromwell? What was his position on the execution of Charles I or the restoration of Charles II?

We do not know the answer to any of these questions. For whatever reason, none of the details of Wilcox's life have been preserved for us. There is no funeral sermon. There is no collection of personal letters. There are no biographical references in the writings of his contemporaries. All that remains of Wilcox is one solitary sermon, entitled *A Guide to Eternal Glory*.[8] Perhaps this is fitting for a man, who (in his own words) was chiefly concerned that Christ should have the preeminence. Undoubtedly, he would have echoed those words that John the Baptist spoke concerning Christ: "He must increase, but I must decrease."[9]

---

Thomas Wilcox (c. 1549–1608). He was an English Puritan, who, along with John Field, published the *Admonition to Parliament* in 1572. It called upon Elizabeth I to complete the reformation of the Church of England by ridding it of all remnants of Roman Catholicism.

6. The Long Parliament was called by Charles I in 1640, in order to pay an indemnity to the Scots after the Bishops' Wars. It was not formally dissolved until 1660.

7. The Court of High Commission was established in 1549, in order to enforce the forms of worship prescribed within the Church of England.

8. The sermon has been published under different titles, including *Christ is All* and *A Choice Drop of Honey from the Rock Christ*. The latter is taken from Ps 81:16, "And with honey out of the rock should I have satisfied thee." Horatius Bonar published an edition, and included a preface along with it. Bonar also included a number of notes in his edition. For a summary of these, see Haykin, "Christ is All," 41–46.

9. John 3:30.

## TO THE READER

In the preamble, entitled "To the Reader,"[10] Wilcox explains why he has published this sermon: "I find in this day many poor souls tossed to and fro, ready to be 'carried about with every wind of doctrine.'"[11] By "every wind of doctrine," he has in mind an unbiblical understanding of justification.[12] For Wilcox, "the way into that pleasant path of soul-justification before God is in and through the righteousness of Jesus Christ."[13] When God justifies sinners, he imputes Christ's righteousness to them. This means that they stand before God, clothed in Christ's righteousness. According to Wilcox, this "pleasant path" is destroyed by those who look to their own righteousness as the grounds of their justification before God.

Wilcox's concern is not unlike that expressed by the apostle Paul in Romans 9:30—10:4. Here, Paul commends the Jews on account of their "zeal for God," while lamenting their lack of "knowledge."[14] They are convinced of their ability to please God by their own effort; therefore, they seek to "establish" their own righteousness.[15] In doing so, they ignore "God's righteousness."[16] Paul makes it clear that God's righteousness is Christ, who is "the end of the law for righteousness to everyone that believeth."[17] What

---

10. Wilcox, *Guide to Eternal Glory*, 1-2.

11. Wilcox, *Guide to Eternal Glory*, 1. Here, Wilcox quotes Eph 4:14, "That we henceforth be no more children, tossed to and fro, and carried about with every wind of doctrine, by the sleight of men, and cunning craftiness, whereby they lie in wait to deceive." See Heb 13:9, for a similar thought.

12. When it comes to the doctrine of justification, Wilcox stands within the mainstream of English Reformed theology. See *The Westminster Confession of Faith*, 11.1, and *The 1689 Baptist Confession*, 11.1. According to the "classical" position, the formal cause of justification is the righteousness of Christ imputed (or reckoned) to those who are made one with him. This position differs from the Council of Trent, which defines justification as the inherent righteousness of the regenerate infused into them. It also differs from the view, popularized by Richard Baxter, according to which "Christ himself fulfilled the conditions of the old covenant, and thereby purchased for us easier terms within the new covenant. On account of Christ's righteousness, our own righteousness (faith and repentance) is accounted, or imputed, as acceptable righteousness. We are, in other words, justified by our own righteousness on account of the righteousness of Christ" (Allison, *Rise of Moralism*, 156-57).

13. Wilcox, *Guide to Eternal Glory*, 1.

14. Rom 10:2.

15. Rom 10:3.

16. Rom 10:3.

17. Rom 10:4.

does that mean? (1) It means that Christ paid the law's penalty. He died as our substitute, bearing the curse of the law. Because our sin is imputed to Christ, God forgives us. (2) It means that Christ obeyed the law's precepts. He lived as our substitute, fulfilling the requirements of the law. Because Christ's righteousness is imputed to us, God declares us *righteous*.[18]

According to Paul, the Jews refuse to subject themselves to this righteousness.[19] As a result, they stumble over Christ.[20] God declares, "Behold, I lay in Zion a stumbling stone and rock of offence: and whosoever believeth on him shall not be ashamed."[21] The Old Testament context is the Assyrian invasion of Israel. The prophet Isaiah declares that Assyria is going to sweep over Israel like a flood. The only place of refuge will be found in God. He will be a rock in the midst of the oncoming flood. For those who trust in anything other than God to save them from the Assyrians, God will become a cause of offense; that is, the floodwaters will sweep them against him to be destroyed. Paul applies that prophecy to Christ. All those who believe in Christ (the rock) are saved from the floodwaters of God's judgment. But all those who do not believe in Christ strike against him. As a result, he becomes "a stumbling stone and rock of offence." According to Paul, this is what has happened to the Jews.

Wilcox is concerned that many in his day make the same mistake as the Jews, in that they too refuse to subject themselves to God's righteousness,[22]

---

18. N. T. Wright openly rejects the "classical" doctrine of the imputation of Christ's righteousness to sinners in *What Saint Paul Really Said*. For a reply, see Piper's *Future of Justification*. Wright's position is not new. As John Owen observes, "Controversies in religion make a great appearance of being new, when they are only varied and made different by the new terms and expressions that are introduced into the handling of them" (*Works*, 5:289). Owen further remarks, "I shall take boldness, therefore, to say, whoever be offended at it, that if we lose the ancient doctrine of justification through faith in the blood of Christ, and the imputation of his righteousness unto us, public profession of religion will quickly issue in Popery or Atheism, or in at least in what is the next door unto it" (*Works*, 5:206–7).

19. Rom 10:3. Thomas Schreiner summarizes the Jews' misunderstanding of the nature of God's righteousness as follows: "They did not subject themselves to God's saving gift of righteousness because they were ignorant that righteousness is a divine gift. This ignorance led them to the vain pursuit of trying to establish their own righteousness—a righteousness based on 'doing' (Rom. 9:32; 10:5) instead of believing (Rom. 9:32–33; 10:6–13). Here Paul counters a form of works-righteousness by which the Jews thought they could attain right standing with God" (*Law and Its Fulfillment*, 134).

20. Rom 9:32.

21. Rom 9:33. Here Paul quotes Isa 8:13–15 and 28:16.

22. Rom 10:3.

trusting instead in their own righteousness. In short, they have a skewed understanding of the doctrine of justification. That is the "wind of doctrine" that Wilcox views as threatening the church. His purpose is to show its folly, and to point his readers to the "pleasant path of soul-justification before God." His approach can be divided into three sections:[23] (1) A call to examine self; (2) a call to combat despair; and (3) a call to consider Christ.

## A CALL TO EXAMINE SELF

Having stated his purpose in the preamble, Wilcox begins by calling his readers to examine themselves: "Try and examine with the greatest strictness every day what bottom your profession and hope of glory is built upon, whether it was laid by the hand of Christ."[24] For Wilcox, self-deception is an ever-present danger. For this reason, people must look seriously at the foundation of their hope. He encourages them to ask, "What righteousness is it that I stand upon to be saved by? Have I got off all my self-righteousness?"[25] Wilcox knows that man's natural tendency is to look to *self* for the grounds of justification.[26] As for the reason why, he explains later in his sermon, "Self-righteousness and self-sufficiency are the darlings of nature, which

---

23. This threefold division is mine (not Wilcox's), yet it seems to be an accurate reflection of the thought-flow in his sermon.

24. Wilcox, *Guide to Eternal Glory*, 2. Wilcox follows this exhortation with an appeal to Christ's warning in Matt 7:27, "The rain descended, and the floods came, and the winds blew, and beat upon that house: and it fell: and great was the fall of it." He takes this verse as a warning that a careless "profession" (a term he uses repeatedly in this section) will issue in ruin. This concern is characteristic of the Puritans in general. For this reason, they place great importance on self-examination. John Owen explains, "The negligence and sloth of many professors can never enough be bewailed. They walk at all adventure, as if there were no devil to tempt them, no world to seduce, ensnare, or oppose them, no treachery in their own hearts to deceive them" (*Exposition of Hebrews*, 4:101). The need for such vigilance is confirmed throughout Scripture. By way of example, see Heb 2:1–4; 3:12—4:13; 5:11—6:20; and 10:19–39.

25. Wilcox, *Guide to Eternal Glory*, 3.

26. It is interesting to note that the apostle Paul points to humility as a certain result of justification. He asks, "Where is boasting then? It is excluded. By what law? Of works? Nay: but by the law of faith. Therefore we conclude that a man is justified by faith without the deeds of the law" (Rom 3:27). In the first part of this verse, the word *law* means *principle*. Thus, Paul is saying that we are not justified by a principle of works, but by a principle of faith. Works are meritorious, in that they merit payment. Faith is not meritorious, in that it does not merit anything. It is simply the means by which the sinner receives God's gift of justification. "Where is boasting then?"

she preserves as her life."²⁷ Again, he states: "If nature had been responsible to contrive the way of salvation, it would have put it into any hands of saints or angels, to sell it, rather than into the hands of Christ, who gives freely, whom therefore it suspects. It would have set up a way to purchase by doing. Therefore, it abominates the merits of Christ, as a destructive thing to it. It would do anything to be saved, rather than to go to Christ, or close with Christ. Christ will have nothing, but the soul will force something of its own upon Christ. Here is the great controversy."²⁸

People want to glory in their own righteousness as the cause of their justification before God. This makes it extremely difficult for them to submit to God's righteousness. "It is," says Wilcox, "the hardest thing in the world to take Christ alone for righteousness."²⁹ But that is exactly what people must do in order to be saved. For this reason, Wilcox pleads with his readers to examine the object of their faith: "If ever you did see Christ, you saw him a Rock, higher than self-righteousness, Satan, sin (Ps. 61:2), and the Rock does follow you (1 Cor. 10:4), and there will be continual droppings of honey and grace out of that Rock to satisfy you (Ps. 81:16). Examine, if ever you did behold Christ as the only-begotten of the Father, full of grace and truth (John 1:14–17). Be sure you have come to Christ, have stood upon the Rock of Ages, have answered his call to your soul, and have closed with him for justification."³⁰

For Wilcox, such a closing with Christ for justification must flow from heartfelt conviction for sin, for that is the only way to be rid of self-righteousness. "To believing," he writes, "there must go a clear conviction of sin, and of the merits of the blood of Christ, and of Christ's willingness to save upon this consideration merely, that you are a sinner; things all harder than to make a world."³¹ Wilcox's point is this: only a deep sense of sin can soften and humble the heart, thereby preparing the way for faith.³² That is

---

27. Wilcox, *Guide to Eternal Glory*, 9. In his discussion of man's corruption, Wilcox makes it clear that Christ is "ugly" to nature. For this reason, "nature cannot desire him." This provides the backdrop for his understanding of the bondage of the will: "Christ is too high and glorious for nature so much as to touch. There must be a divine nature first put into the soul to make it lay hold of him" (*Guide to Eternal Glory*, 10). Here, Wilcox's Reformed convictions are evident.

28. Wilcox, *Guide to Eternal Glory*, 7.

29. Ibid., 4.

30. Ibid., 3–4.

31. Ibid., 4.

32. This must not be confused with preparationism, according to which people must

precisely what he wants his readers to look for in themselves. If they have never been fully convinced of their absolute sinfulness before God and of their utter inability to please him, then they have never let go of their self-righteousness.[33] And if they have never let go of their self-righteousness, then they have never closed with Christ by faith.

Wilcox's conviction is a central Puritan motif. According to William Perkins, "the preparation of the heart is by humbling and softening."[34] This is accomplished through various means:[35] "the knowledge of the word of God;" "the sight of sin arising of the knowledge of the law;" "a sorrow for sin, which is a pain and pricking in the heart arising of the feeling of the displeasure of God;" and "an holy desperation: which is, when a man is wholly out of all hope ever to attain salvation by any strength or good of his own." When people's hearts are humbled and softened in this way, they become, in the words of Richard Sibbes, "bruised reeds."[36] By this, he means that they become conscious of their sin and mindful of their need. For Sibbes, "This bruising is required before conversion so that the Spirit may make way for himself into the heart by levelling all proud, high thoughts, and that we may understand ourselves to be what indeed we are by nature."[37] The Puritans equate this "bruising" with the proclamation of God's law. In brief, the Holy Spirit applies the law to sinners whereby they are convinced that it is speaking against them.

---

fulfill certain requirements before believing. For the most part, the Puritans are careful to acknowledge that conviction for sin varies in degree and expression from person to person. The issue is not external expressions of sorrow, but whether or not people are convinced that their righteousness is as "filthy rags" in God's sight (Isa 64:6). Flavel provides a helpful warning against preparationism: "I pity many poor souls upon this account, who stand off from Christ, dare not believe because they want such and such qualifications to fit them for Christ. Oh, saith one, could I find so much brokenness of heart for sin, so much reformation and power over corruptions, then I could come to Christ; the meaning of which is this, if I could bring a price in my hand to purchase him, then I should be encouraged to go unto him. Here now lies horrible pride covered over with a veil of great humility" (*Works*, 4:57).

33. It is worth noting that very few people object to being told that they do *bad* things. However, everyone objects to being told that they never do any *good* things. They hold tenaciously to their self-righteousness. Wilcox's point is that they must let go of this very thing in order to be saved.

34. Perkins, *Treatise Tending*, 1:363.

35. Ibid., 1:363–65.

36. Sibbes, *Bruised Reed*, 3. See Matt 12:20.

37. Sibbes, *Bruised Reed*, 4.

This process is exemplified in the apostle Paul, who writes, "For I was alive without the law once: but when the commandment came, sin revived, and I died."[38] Here, Paul describes life and death in relative terms. Basically, there was a time when he was alive apart from the law. He had studied it since childhood, yet he lacked any experiential knowledge of it. Without that experiential knowledge, he felt alive. In other words, he thought all was well with his soul: "[I] profited in the Jews' religion above many my equals in mine own nation, being more exceedingly zealous of the traditions of my fathers."[39] Elsewhere he says of himself, "Touching the righteousness which is in the law, blameless."[40] However, the time came when he died. Why? The law arrived home, and sin became alive. In other words, the law revealed and provoked his sin. He saw God's righteousness and holiness. As a result, he saw the depths of his own depravity. The law killed him, making him utterly weak. In a word, he became a "bruised reed."

Once the heart experiences such "humbling and softening," it is ready for faith. Perkins says, God "causeth faith by little and little to spring and to breed in the heart."[41] Essentially, the Holy Spirit "makes" the sinner (1) "to ponder most diligently the great mercy of God offered unto him in Christ Jesus," (2) "to see, feel, and from his heart to acknowledge himself to stand in need of Christ," (3) to "desire" Christ, and (4) to cry with the publican, "O God be merciful to me a sinner."[42] At this point, people look to Christ for salvation. "In this order," writes John Flavel, "the Spirit (ordinarily) draws souls to Christ, he shines into their minds by illumination; applies that light to their consciences by effectual conviction; breaks and wounds their hearts for sin by compunction; and then moves the will to embrace and close with Christ in the way of faith for life and salvation."[43]

Wilcox stands in the Puritan mainstream. He believes that "whatever is of nature's spinning must be all unravelled before the righteousness of Christ can be put on."[44] People must be convinced that "nature can afford no balsam

---

38. Rom 7:9.
39. Gal 1:14.
40. Phil 3:6.
41. Perkins, *Treatise Tending*, 1:363.
42. Ibid., 1:365. See Luke 18:13.
43. Flavel, *Works*, 2:71. People will not rest in God's mercy in Christ until they are convinced of their utter sinfulness. Concerning the essential relationship between conviction for sin and faith in Christ, Owen remarks, "Until men know themselves better, they will care very little to know Christ at all" (*Works*, 5:21).
44. Wilcox, *Guide to Eternal Glory*, 3.

fit for soul-cure... Poor ragged nature, with all its highest improvements, can never spin a garment fine enough (without spot) or large enough (without patches) to cover the soul's nakedness. Nothing can fit the soul for that use but Christ's perfect righteousness."[45] Once convinced of this, people renounce their self-righteousness, and close with Christ, presenting nothing but their "sin and misery."[46] For Wilcox, this is the nature of true saving faith. And it is this faith that he longs for his readers to find in themselves.

## A CALL TO COMBAT DESPAIR

Following his description of what it means to believe, Wilcox considers what it is that dissuades some people from closing with Christ for justification. In a word, it is despair. Because of their guilt, they doubt God's willingness to forgive. Because they doubt God's willingness to forgive, they refuse to believe. "Where guilt is," writes Wilcox, "there is hardness of heart."[47] The only solution for such despair is Christ. He is our Advocate, Surety, and Mediator.[48] Furthermore, he "is our temple, sacrifice, altar, and high-priest also, to whom none must come but sinners, and that without any offering but his own blood once offered (Heb. 7:27)."[49] Wilcox makes it clear that it is Christ's entrance into God's presence that guarantees the sinner's acceptance with God.[50] For this reason, those who despair must look to Christ. "In all the Scripture," writes Wilcox, "there is not an ill word against

---

45. Ibid., 3. The Puritans believe that the doctrine of justification rises or falls with the doctrine of sin. James White expresses this same conviction as follows: "Change the biblical teaching of man's need, and you will of necessity have to change the nature of the salvation God provides. Every fundamental error regarding the doctrine of justification that man has ever invented flows from a denial of the nature and impact of sin in man's life. Indeed, when one allows man to make any kind of response to God, to cling to any shred of self-righteousness, the result will always be an addition to faith alone as the means of justification" (*God Who Justifies*, 51).

46. Wilcox, *Guide to Eternal Glory*, 9. Elsewhere, he states, "The greatness of Christ's merits is not known but to a poor soul at the greatest loss. Slight convictions will have but slight, low prizing of Christ's blood and merits" (*Guide to Eternal Glory*, 8).

47. Ibid., 5.

48. Ibid., 5. See Gal 3:20; 1 Tim 2:5; Heb 7:20–22; and 1 John 2:1.

49. Wilcox, *Guide to Eternal Glory*, 6. He seems to have summarized the entire Book of Hebrews in this single statement.

50. John Owen comments, "It is generally acknowledged that sinners could not be saved without the death of Christ; but that believers could not be saved without the life of Christ following it, is not so much considered" (*Exposition of Hebrews*, 5:542).

a poor sinner, stripped of self-righteousness."[51] Christ invites such as these to come to him. Wilcox reenforces this invitation with two exhortations.

First, he exhorts his readers to "remember all the patterns of grace that are in heaven."[52] The greatest of these is Christ's blood, which points to reconciliation, cleansing, redemption, remission, liberty, justification, and nearness to God.[53] When tempted to despair, people must look to Christ's blood, and remember that "the greatest sinner did never pose the grace of Christ."[54]

Second, Wilcox exhorts his readers to "look more at justification than sanctification."[55] In other words, it is important to remember that justification, not sanctification, is the grounds of our acceptance with God. In affirming this, Wilcox does not deny the importance of looking at sanctification to see the evidence of God's grace at work. His concern is simply that such self-examination should never become the foundation of the Christian's hope. He declares, "Graces may be evidences, but only the merits of Christ must be the foundation for your hope to bottom on."[56]

Wilcox's remarks raise the controversial issue of the Puritan doctrine of assurance. According to *The Westminster Confession of Faith*, assurance is founded upon (1) "the divine truth of the promises of salvation," (2) "the inward evidence of those graces unto which these promises are made," and (3) "the testimony of the Spirit of adoption witnessing with our spirits that we are the children of God."[57] Thomas Watson explains this threefold ground of assurance as follows: "Assurance consists of a practical syllogism, in which the Word of God makes the major, conscience the minor, and the Spirit of God the conclusion. The Word says, 'He that fears and loves God is loved of God'; there is the major proposition; then conscience makes the minor, 'But I fear and love God'; then the Spirit makes the conclusion, 'Therefore thou art loved of God'; and this is what the apostle calls 'The witnessing of the Spirit with our spirits, that we are his children.'"[58]

---

51. Wilcox, *Guide to Eternal Glory*, 6. See Matt 11:28 and 12:20.

52. Wilcox, *Guide to Eternal Glory*, 6.

53. Ibid., 6. See Col 1:20; 1 John 1:7; Acts 20:28; 1 Pet 1:18–19; Heb 9:13–14; 9:22; 10:19; Rom 5:9; and Eph 2:13.

54. Wilcox, *Guide to Eternal Glory*, 6.

55. Ibid., 7.

56. Iibd., 7.

57. *The Westminster Confession of Faith*, 18.2. *The 1689 Baptist Confession*, 18.2, makes the same threefold appeal.

58. Watson, *Body of Divinity*, 174. See Rom 8:16.

Essentially, this means that the Holy Spirit impresses the reality of the marks of grace upon Christians, thereby assuring them that they are partakers in the promises of Scripture.[59] In commenting on the Puritan understanding of Romans 8:16,[60] James Packer writes, "The Puritans identified 'our spirit' with the Christian's conscience, which, with the Spirit's aid, is able to discern in his heart the marks which Scripture specifies as tokens of the new birth and to conclude from them that he is a child of God."[61] In this paradigm, the Holy Spirit both provides the evidence (i.e., the marks of grace) and empowers the individual's reason to evaluate it. Turning to 2 Corinthians 13:5[62] and 2 Peter 1:10,[63] the Puritans urge Christians to examine their lives to find the evidence of God's work. This self-examination is known as "the reflex act of faith."

A misuse of the Puritan doctrine of assurance opens the door to three potential dangers.[64] The first is introspection. The Puritans frequently

59. The Puritans agree as to the first two grounds of assurance but not the third. Joel Beeke identifies three schools of thought. (1) Some view the testimony of the Holy Spirit as referring exclusively to the practical and mystical syllogisms. (2) Some distinguish the Holy Spirit witnessing with the Christian's spirit by syllogism from his witnessing to the Christian's spirit by direct applications of the Word. (3) Some believe the witness of the Holy Spirit is an immediate impression which marked the zenith of the experimental life—often equated with the "sealing of the Spirit" (Eph 1:13) ("Personal Assurance of Faith," 25–27).

60. "The Spirit itself beareth witness with our spirit, that we are the children of God."

61. Packer, *Quest for Godliness*, 183.

62. "Examine yourselves, whether ye be in the faith; prove your own selves."

63. "Wherefore the rather, brethren, give diligence to make your calling and election sure: for if ye do these things, ye shall never fall."

64. These potential dangers have led some to reject the Puritan doctrine of assurance. Michael Eaton, for example, states, "If Christ did not die for all, and if it is possible to have a sorrow for sin which is not true repentance, a faith which is not true faith, a possessing of the Spirit which falls short of true regeneration, if despite any and every 'experience' of the gospel there is 'a way to Hell even from the Gates of Heaven,' if Paul himself feared loss of salvation, then what remains of the Calvinist's assurance? It has died the death of a thousand qualifications" (*No Condemnation*, 23). By way of solution, he states, "The essence of the theology which I wish to explore is that salvation and good works are not inexorably tied together" (*No Condemnation*, 39). In other words, there is no definite correlation between justification and sanctification. He explains, "One's justified-regenerate position in Christ enables progress in godly living, demands such progress, inspires it, and has a tendency which leads powerfully in that direction. That it inexorably and invariably produces godliness however must be questioned" (*No Condemnation*, 168). His entire thesis builds on the earlier work of R. T. Kendall, who asserts that the Westminster divines depart from Calvin's belief that "faith is *knowledge* . . . merely witnessing what God has already done in Christ" and that assurance is "the

compel their readers to examine themselves. If people are not careful, such self-examination can quickly turn into gloomy introspection. Andrew Davies sees the danger, commenting, "Whilst their stress on self-examination was a healthy corrective to those who were in danger of hypocrisy, it was an unhelpful emphasis for those who were given to introspection."[65] The second danger is despair. While affirming the need for warm affections as a sign of God's grace, the Puritans acknowledge that many people suffer from cold affections. By way of solution, they often propose that dissatisfaction with one's lack of affection is a sign of affection.[66] Such reasoning can easily lead to a vicious cycle whereby anxiety becomes a mark of piety. The third danger is legalism. The Puritans' emphasis upon "marks" is susceptible to being misconstrued as a works-oriented concept of salvation. Whenever detailed instructions for obedience become central, God's grace is eventually threatened.

These "potential" dangers (particularly the second) appear to be behind Wilcox's appeal "to look more at justification than sanctification."[67]

---

direct act of faith" (*Calvin and English Calvinism*, 19–20, 25). Both Eaton and Kendall contend that faith yields justification without necessarily yielding good works. According to this way of thinking, faith is a simple profession, whereby a person gives *mental* assent to the gospel. Surely, this is the very thing that is denounced in Jas 2:14–26. In this connection, Owen writes, "We are justified by faith alone; but we are not justified by that faith which can be alone. Alone, respects its influence into our justification, not its nature and existence. And we absolutely deny that we can be justified by that faith which can be alone; that is, without a principle of spiritual life and universal obedience, operative in all the works of it, as duty doth require . . . We allow no faith to be of the same kind or nature with that whereby we are justified, but what virtually and radically contains in it universal obedience, as the effect is in the cause, the fruit in the root . . ." (*Works*, 5:73).

65. Davies, "The Holy Spirit in Puritan Experience," 25.

66. At one point, Swinnock encourages his readers "to weep over thy tears, to be ashamed of thy shame, and to abhor thyself for thy self-abhorrency" (*Works*, 1:190). In isolation, such an exhortation could lead to a never ending cycle of despair. However, it must not be wrenched from the context of Swinnock's complete works. See my comments in the next footnote.

67. The vast majority of the Puritans agree with Wilcox. The notion that they advocate introspection, leading to a gloomy state of despair, arises when people fail to grasp two essential features of their call to self-examination. (1) The Puritans are not so concerned about imparting assurance as they are about awakening a sleepy generation of churchgoers from their false sense of security. They are keenly aware of the danger of *civility* or *morality* (i.e., trusting in the external forms of religion). As R. C. Lovelace explains, "The problem that confronts the Puritans as they look out on their decaying society and their lukewarm church is not simply to dislodge the faithful from the slough of mortal or venial sin, but radically to awaken those who are professing but not actual Christians, who are caught in a trap of carnal security" ("The Anatomy of Puritan Piety," 303). (2)

Evidently, he knows of some who have succumbed to despair, because they have attempted to find in their sanctification the grounds of their acceptance with God rather than the evidence of God's grace at work. They have come away empty because they have lost sight of God, "who justifies the ungodly."[68] For this reason, Wilcox warns, "Labor after sanctification to your utmost, but make not a Christ of it to save you. If so, it must come down one way or other. Christ's infinite satisfaction, not your sanctification, must be your justification before God."[69] Clearly, for Wilcox, the call to self-examination and the pursuit of sanctification must never be divorced from a wholehearted adherence to the doctrine of justification by grace alone through faith alone in Christ alone. He writes:

> When we come to God, we must bring nothing but Christ with us. Any ingredients of our own qualifications will poison and corrupt faith. He who builds upon duties, graces, etc. knows not the merits of Christ. This makes believing so hard, so far above nature. If you believe, you must every day renounce (as dung and dross (Phil. 3:7–8)) your privileges, your obedience, your sanctification, your duties, your graces, your tears, your meltings, your humiliations, and nothing but Christ must be held up. Every day, your workings, your self-sufficiency must be destroyed. You must take all out of God's hand. Christ is the gift of God (John 4:10). Faith is the gift of God (Eph. 2:8). Pardon is a free gift (Rom. 5:16). Ah, how nature storms, frets, and rages at this; that all is of gift, and it can

---

The Puritans do not divorce the practice of self-examination from their proclamation of the doctrine of justification. By way of example, in his treatise, *The Touchstone of Sincerity* (*Works*, 2:328–421), Flavel seeks to distinguish between true and nominal Christians. If this treatise is read in isolation, then it could lead people into an unhelpful state of introspection. However, it must not be separated from what Flavel says concerning "the transcendent excellency of Jesus Christ" in *The Fountain of Life: A Display of Christ in His Essential and Mediatorial Glory* (*Works*, 1:3–561). When the Puritans are read in their entirety, it is evident that they echo Wilcox's conviction that justification is the only grounds of the Christian's hope.

68. Rom 4:5. Many people search within for a reason why God should justify them, but they never find it. God does not justify the sanctified; he sanctifies the justified. It is important to never lose sight of that order. When people do, they fall prey to legalism. They begin to think that there must be something in them that accounts for their justification.

69. Wilcox, *Guide to Eternal Glory*, 10. Wilcox does not divorce justification and sanctification. Both of these blessings flow from union with Christ. They are distinct, yet inseparable. All whom God justifies, He sanctifies. Wilcox's point is simply this: we must look to justification alone as the basis of our hope before God.

purchase nothing with its own actions, and tears, and duties; that all its works are excluded, and of no value in heaven!⁷⁰

Repeatedly, Wilcox stresses the fact that people must renounce every last vestige of self-righteousness and look at Christ alone for "the least sight of him will be saving."⁷¹ He gives two reasons why. The first is Christ's meekness: "He will do that himself which he requires of his creature . . . He will forgive, not only seven times, but seventy times seven."⁷² The second is Christ's atonement: "He has drunk the bitterness of the cup, and left you the sweet; the condemnation is out. Christ drank up all the Father's wrath at one draught, and nothing but salvation is left for you."⁷³ In Wilcox's estimation, such a view of Christ is the only source of relief for a soul in the grip of despair.

## A CALL TO CONSIDER CHRIST

Wilcox's plea to look at Christ alone, for "the least sight of him will be saving," becomes the focus of the remainder of his sermon. Essentially, he provides a series of exhortations that explain what it means to consider Christ.⁷⁴ They can be grouped under four main headings.

### Applying Christ's Blood

For starters, to look at Christ is to apply Christ's blood. Wilcox exhorts his readers, "Keep always a humble, empty, broken frame of heart, sensible of any spiritual miscarriage, observant of all inward workings, fit for the highest communications."⁷⁵ This "broken frame of heart" is exemplified in Christ's words in Matthew 5:3, "Blessed are the poor in spirit: for their's

---

70. Ibid., 7.
71. Ibid., 8.
72. Ibid., 8. See Matt 18:21–22.
73. Wilcox, *Guide to Eternal Glory*, 9. While on the cross, Christ declares, "It is finished" (John 19:30). What is finished? Christ says, "My meat is to do the will of him that sent me, and to finish his work" (John 4:34). Again, "I have glorified thee on the earth: I have finished the work which thou gavest me to do" (John 17:4). This means that God's work is finished. Christ has given his life for the sheep (John 10:11). The penalty is paid, the curse is removed, and the devil is defeated.
74. There are at least sixty exhortations on pages 11–15.
75. Wilcox, *Guide to Eternal Glory*, 11.

## Looking unto Jesus

is the kingdom of heaven." Poverty of spirit is an attitude before God that arises from a proper self-perception. People perceive their sin, recognizing that they are without moral virtues adequate to commend themselves to God. As a result, they are aware of their utter dependence upon God's grace. William Perkins expresses it like this: "Finding no goodness in their hearts, they despair in themselves, and fly wholly to the mercy of God in Christ, for grace and comfort."[76] Similarly, in defining the poor in spirit, Thomas Watson refers to "those who are brought to the sense of their sins, and seeing no goodness in themselves, despair in themselves and sue wholly to the mercy of God in Christ."[77]

According to the Puritans, true poverty of spirit always leads to Christ. Wilcox makes the same point. To the above exhortation, he adds the following: "Keep not guilt in the conscience, but apply the blood of Christ immediately. God charges sin and guilt upon you, to make you look to Christ the brazen serpent."[78] In other words, people should always seek to cultivate a "humble, empty, broken frame of heart," while remembering that Christ came to save the ungodly and unrighteous—those who put no confidence in the flesh.[79] Wilcox is aware that many people err at this very point. They think they must fulfill certain conditions necessary for justification—they must be sad enough, earnest enough, holy enough, or good enough. Or they think they must be sufficiently diligent in the performance of spiritual duties. Unsurprisingly, they begin to wallow in their unworthiness.[80] For Wilcox, their problem is rooted in pride. He declares in very pointed terms: "You complain much of yourself. Does your sin make you look more at Christ, less at self? That is right, else complaining is but hypocrisy. To

---

76. Perkins, *Sermon on the Mount*, 3:4.
77. Watson, *Beatitudes*, 42.
78. Wilcox, *Guide to Eternal Glory*, 11.
79. Phil 3:3.
80. When people wallow in their perceived unworthiness, they have lost sight of what is made so evident in Scripture: God justifies the ungodly (Rom 4:5). The Bible is full of encouraging examples. Noah became drunk, yet he "found grace in the eyes of the LORD" (Gen 11:8). Abraham was willing to sacrifice his wife's honor by telling the Egyptians that she was his sister, yet "he was called 'the friend of God'" (Jas 2:23). Jacob deceived his father and brother, yet God declares, "I am the God of Jacob" (Exod 3:15). Moses murdered an Egyptian, yet God states, "With him will I speak mouth to mouth" (Num 12:8). David committed adultery and murder, yet God says that David was a "man after his own heart" (1 Sam 13:14). These examples confirm what David celebrates in Ps 32:2, "Blessed is the man unto whom the LORD imputeth not iniquity." Also see Rom 4:6–8.

be looking at duties, graces, enlargements, when you should be looking at Christ, that is pitiful."[81]

To look at Christ is to apply his blood. It is to live in the light of what the apostle Paul declares in Romans 5:1, "Therefore being justified by faith, we have peace with God through our Lord Jesus Christ." The term *peace* means binding together what has been separated. Believers are bound together with God by Christ's blood.[82] That is made clear in Hebrews 9:14, "How much more shall the blood of Christ, who through the eternal Spirit offered himself without spot to God, purge your conscience from dead works to serve the living God?" According to this verse, the value of Christ's blood is twofold. First, it is offered to God. This means that it makes atonement for sin; it satisfies God's justice, appeases God's wrath, and secures God's mercy. Second, it cleanses the conscience from dead works. The expression "dead works" refers to sin's guilt and defilement. How is the conscience cleansed from dead works? The guilt of sin is removed by Christ's blood (justification), and the defilement of sin is removed by Christ's blood (sanctification).

Wilcox pleads with his readers to remember that this blood is in heaven, and that "not a drop . . . will be lost."[83] The blood of the Old Testament sacrifices was carried repeatedly into an "earthly" sanctuary,[84] but the blood of Christ has entered heaven once for all. For this reason, the author of Hebrews declares, "Having therefore, brethren, boldness to enter into the holiest by the blood of Jesus . . . let us draw near with a true heart in full assurance of faith, having our hearts sprinkled from an evil conscience, and our bodies washed with pure water."[85] In a word, Christ's atonement is complete. Therefore, believers must, in the words of Wilcox, "keep the eye constantly upon Christ's blood."[86]

## Seeking Christ's Presence

For Wilcox, to look at Christ also means to seek his presence. He makes it clear that Christ is found in spiritual duties such as praying, receiving the Lord's Supper, and hearing God's Word. In typical Puritan fashion, he refers

81. Wilcox, *Guide to Eternal Glory*, 6.
82. Rom 5:9.
83. Wilcox, *Guide to Eternal Glory*, 6.
84. Heb 9:24–25.
85. Heb 10:19, 22.
86. Wilcox, *Guide to Eternal Glory*, 14.

to these as "glorious ordinances."[87] They are the means through which God imparts grace to the soul. He would agree with Swinnock, who describes spiritual duties as "conduit-pipes whereby the water of life is derived from Christ in the hearts of Christians."[88] This concept is pivotal to Puritan piety. Lewis Bayly affirms that the essence of piety is "to join together, in watching, fasting, praying, reading the Scriptures, keeping his Sabbaths, hearing sermons, receiving the holy Communion, relieving the poor, exercising in all humility the works of piety to God, and walking conscionably in the duties of our calling towards men."[89]

While placing tremendous importance on the practice of spiritual duties, the Puritans are aware of the danger that arises when such practice is divorced from the pursuit of Christ. They make it clear that duties are not an end in themselves; rather, they are a means to an end—communion with Christ. Christians must not be satisfied in the mere performance of spiritual duties but in their fellowship with Christ through them. With precisely that in mind, Baxter declares, "Look not so much to the time [you] spend in the duty, as to the quantity and quality of the work that is done."[90]

Wilcox issues the same warning. He urges his readers: "Be serious, exact in duty, having the weight of it upon the heart; but be as much afraid of taking comfort from duties, as of sins. Comfort from any hand but Christ's is deadly."[91] He issues this caution throughout his sermon: "The greatest sins can be hid under the greatest duties";[92] "Healing from duty, and not from Christ, is the most desperate disease";[93] "If you have seen Christ, you would not do a duty without him for ten thousand worlds";[94] "He who builds upon duties, graces, etc. knows not the merits of Christ."[95] Simply put, spiritual duties are useless without Christ. Wilcox actually takes it a step further, affirming that, apart from Christ, they are dangerous, because they can lead to false comfort, false security, and false hope. When they do, they ultimately lead to pride.

87. Ibid., 2.
88. Swinnock, *Works*, 1:102.
89. Bayly, *Practice of Piety*, 163.
90. Baxter, *Practical Works*, 110.
91. Wilcox, *Guide to Eternal Glory*, 11.
92. Ibid., 3.
93. Ibid.
94. Ibid.
95. Ibid., 7.

For this reason, Wilcox encourages his readers to examine themselves, in the performance of duties: "Observe, every day, that you have the dayspring from on high (with his morning dews of mourning for sin) constantly visiting (Luke 1:17), the bright morning-star (with fresh influences of grace and peace) constantly arising (Rev. 22:16), and Christ sweetly greeting the soul in all duties."[96] That must be the goal in every prayer uttered, every sermon enjoyed, and every communion celebrated. "In every duty," declares Wilcox, "look at Christ; before duty to pardon, in duty to assist, and after duty to accept. Without this, it is but carnal, careless duty."[97]

## Prizing Christ's Righteousness

Another important way in which Christians are to look at Christ is by prizing his righteousness. Wilcox writes, "Remember your sins, and Christ's pardonings; your desserts, Christ's merits; your weakness, Christ's strength; your pride, Christ's humility; your many infirmities, Christ's restorings; your guilt, Christ's new application of his blood; your fallings, Christ's raising up; your slightness, Christ's sufferings; your want, Christ's fullness; your temptations, Christ's tenderness; your vileness, Christ's righteousness."[98] All of these blessings belong to Christians by virtue of their union with Christ.[99] In the words of Edward Pearse, this union "is that spiritual conjunction or relation that is between Christ and believers, between the person of Christ and the person of believers, arising from his inhabitation in them by his Spirit and their closing with him by faith."[100] In other words, the Holy Spirit makes Christians one with Christ by virtue of his dwelling in them.

At the outset of his sermon, Wilcox makes reference to a particular metaphor used in Ephesians 4:15[101] to describe this union: the body. Christians stand to Christ in the same relation as the members of a physical body stand to their head, and Christ stands to believers in the same relation as

---

96. Ibid., 13.

97. Ibid., 7.

98. Ibid., 12–13.

99. For more on the Puritan treatment of this important theme, see Yuille, *Inner Sanctum of Puritan Piety*.

100. Pearse, *Best Match*, 4.

101. "From whom the whole body fitly joined together and compacted by that which every joint supplieth, according to the effectual working in the measure of every part, maketh increase of the body unto the edifying of itself in love."

Looking unto Jesus

the head of a physical body stands to its members. What relation is this? Just as the head gives sense and motion to its physical body, Christ gives sense and motion to his mystical body.

As a result of this "intimate conjunction," the body has communion with the head. In other words, Christians have communion with Christ. They share in his names, titles, righteousness, holiness, death, resurrection, and glory. In brief, a great transaction has taken place.[102] This is particularly true of Christ's righteousness. The apostle Paul says, "By him are ye in Christ Jesus, who of God is made unto us . . . righteousness."[103] All those who are in Christ are righteous, because they are *one* with the Righteous One. Christ's righteousness is reckoned to them by virtue of the fact that they are united with him.[104] In the words of Owen:

> Being engrafted into Christ, fastened, united unto him, he makes his things ours, communicates his riches unto us, interposeth his righteousness between the judgment of God and our unrighteousness: and under that, as under a shield and buckler, he hides us from that divine wrath which we have deserved, he defends and protects us therewith; yea, he communicates it unto us and makes it ours, so as that, being covered and adorned therewith, we may boldly and securely place ourselves before the divine tribunal and judgment, so as not only to appear righteous, but so to be.[105]

For Wilcox, to look at Christ is to gaze continually upon his righteousness. It is to remember that we are one with him.[106] What is ours is his: sin.

---

102. Pearse explains, "Behold, whatever Christ is or has, which believers are capable of, is all theirs, and they all hold communion with him therein" (*Best Match*, 10).

103. 1 Cor 1:30.

104. Joseph Hall declares, "What a marvelous and happy exchange is here! We are nothing but sin: Christ is perfect righteousness. He is made our sin that we might be made his righteousness" (*Christ Mystical*, 101). James White comments on the value of this great exchange: "The righteousness that is imputed by faith is Christ's perfect righteousness, and the resulting relationship, secured by the work of the Divine Substitute himself, produces the very peace Paul promised (Rom. 5:1), and all the praise and glory can go solely to God for his work in Christ (*Soli Deo Gloria*). 'Impute' is a small word, but the sin-wearied soul who realizes what it really means finds it to be a true source of hope and constant encouragement" (*God Who Justifies*, 12).

105. Owen, *Doctrine of Justification*, 5:39.

106. We forget this precious truth to our detriment. Christ declares, "I am come that they might have life, and that they might have it more abundantly" (John 10:10). He is not talking about personal peace and affluence, but spiritual life. This life is abundant, because Christ: (1) pays all our debts (Rom 6:23); (2) satisfies all our needs (Col 2:3); (3) carries all our burdens (Heb 4:15); (4) sanctifies all our afflictions (Rom 8:28); (5) defeats

What is his is ours: righteousness. "The more you look at Christ, the Sun of righteousness," writes Wilcox, "the stronger and clearer will the eye of faith be. Look but at Christ, and you will love him and live on him."[107]

## Esteeming Christ's Priesthood

Finally, Wilcox tells his readers to look at Christ by esteeming his priesthood. He exhorts them: "If you be troubled, see Christ your peace (Eph. 2:14), leaving you peace, when he went up to heaven, again and again charging you not to be troubled, no not in the least (sinfully troubled), so as to obstruct your comfort or your believing (John 14:1, 27)."[108] In a word, Christians are to meditate upon this wonderful truth: "We have such a high priest, who is set on the right hand of the throne of the Majesty in the heavens."[109]

Christ's priesthood consists of two parts: oblation (sacrifice) and intercession (prayer). Significantly, they correspond to the high priest's "double office" under the Mosaic covenant, whereby he offered the blood of the sacrifice outside the holy place (oblation) and presented the blood of the sacrifice inside the holy place (intercession). Christ's "oblation" is offered to make atonement by giving God a full and adequate satisfaction for the sins of his people. At the cross, Christ delivered his people from sin by being made sin, and from the curse by being made a curse. As a result, they "have peace with God."[110] The second part of Christ's priesthood is his intercession. In heaven, Christ presents himself before God on behalf of his people. In this way, he guarantees the application of all that he procured by his crucifixion and resurrection.

It is particularly this ministry of intercession that Wilcox has in view when he speaks of Christ's priesthood.[111] As to the actual manner of Christ's

---

all our enemies (1 Cor 15:56–57); and (6) guarantees our inheritance (Rom 8:17).

107. Wilcox, *Guide to Eternal Glory*, 14.

108. Ibid., 15.

109. Heb 8:1. Also see Heb 4:14–16.

110. Rom 5:1. Also see Rom 8:1.

111. There is, in the words of Owen, "a double sacerdotal prayer." (1) There is a prayer that accompanied Christ's oblation (Ps 22:1–3, 15; Matt 26:37; 27:46; Luke 22:44; Heb 5:7). "And this," writes Owen, "having respect unto the justice of God, the curse of the law, and the punishment due to sin, was made in agony, distress, and conflict, with wrestlings, expressed by cries, tears, and most vehement intensions of soul" (*Exposition of Hebrews*, 4:504). (2) There is a prayer that takes place in heaven (John 17:1–26). Having offered his atoning sacrifice, Christ now ensures its efficacy by his intercession: "Wherefore he is able

intercession, John Owen points to three things that take place: (1) "the presentation of his person before the throne of God on our behalf (Heb. 9:24)"; (2) "the representation of his death, oblation, and sacrifice for us; which gives power, life, and efficacy unto his intercession (Rev. 5:6)"; and (3) "a putting up, a requesting, and offering unto God, of his desires and will for the church, attended with care, love, and compassion (Zech. 1:12)."[112] Wilcox does not use these terms, but he has this ministry in mind when he declares, "He is now upon the throne, having spoiled upon his cross (in the lowest state of his humiliation) all whatsoever can hurt or annoy you. He has borne all your sins, sorrows, fears, disgraces, sicknesses, troubles, temptations, and is gone to prepare mansions for you."[113]

The apostle Paul declares, "Who shall lay any thing to the charge of God's elect? It is God that justifieth? Who is he that condemneth? It is Christ that died, yea rather, that is risen again, who is even at the right hand of God, who also maketh intercession for us?"[114] Here Paul mentions three inseparable works. The first is Christ's crucifixion: he "died." In so doing, he paid the penalty for our sin. The second is Christ's resurrection: he has "risen again." This testifies to God's acceptance of Christ's substitutionary sacrifice. The third is Christ's intercession: he "maketh intercession for us." His presence in heaven guarantees the application of all he accomplished by his death, burial, and resurrection.

With Christ's intercessory work in view, Wilcox exhorts, "See Christ praying for you, using his interest with the Father for you."[115] He is thinking in particular of Christ's high-priestly prayer, as recorded in John 17.[116]

---

to save them to the uttermost that come unto God by him, seeing he ever liveth to make intercession for them" (Heb 7:25). Commenting on this verse, Owen writes, "And as the fire on the altar kindled all the renewed sacrifices, which were to be repeated and multiplied, because of their weakness and imperfection; so doth the intercession of Christ make effectual the one perfect sacrifice which he offered once for all, in the various applications of it unto the consciences of believers (Heb. 10:2)" (*Exposition of Hebrews*, 5:538).

112. Owen, *Exposition of Hebrews*, 5:541.
113. Wilcox, *Guide to Eternal Glory*, 15. See John 14:2.
114. Rom 8:33–34.
115. Wilcox, *Guide to Eternal Glory*, 15.
116. In chapters 13–17, John records Christ's private ministry: "Having loved his own which were in the world, he loved them unto the end" (John 13:1). Christ speaks *to* us from God in chapters 13–16, and speaks *for* us to God in chapter 17. In John 17:6–10, Christ provides a detailed description of his people. (1) They know God's name (verse 6). (2) They are recipients of God's grace (v. 6). (3) They keep God's word (v. 7). (4) They believe in Christ (vv. 7–8). (5) They glorify Christ (v. 9).

(1) Christ prays, "Holy Father, keep through thine own name those whom thou hast given me."[117] The Father keeps us from the "evil one" and the "world."[118] (2) Christ prays, "Sanctify them through thy truth: thy word is truth."[119] He makes it clear that we are not "of the world" even as he was not "of the world,"[120] yet we are sent "into the world" even as he was sent "into the world."[121] For this reason, he asks his Father to set us apart. (3) Christ prays, "Father, I will that they also, whom thou hast given me, be with me where I am, that they may behold my glory, which thou hast given me."[122] In interpreting this request, we must remember that it is possible to see Christ in three ways. First, it is possible to see him *carnally* with the eye of flesh. That is true of all who saw him while he was on earth. Second, it is possible to see him *fiducially* with the eye of faith. That is true of all who believe in him: "And this is the will of him that sent me, that every one which seeth the Son, and believeth on him, may have everlasting life: and I will raise him up at the last day."[123] Third, it is possible to see him *beatifically* with the eye of glory. That is also true of all who believe in him: "And though after my skin worms destroy this body, yet in my flesh shall I see God: Whom I shall see for myself, and mine eyes shall behold, and not another."[124] That is what Christ has in view, when he prays that we might "behold" him.

For Wilcox, this entire prayer is a source of great encouragement. Christ has ascended to the right hand of the Father. He has seized heaven as our right. He has entered heaven as our advocate. His Father has glorified him, in answer to his prayer.[125] (1) Christ asked the Father to glorify him by

---

117. John 17:5, 11.

118. John 17:14-15. Thomas Manton remarks, "The world is Satan's chessboard; we can hardly move back or forth but the devil sets out one creature or another to attack us, either by fear, causing us to draw back, or by the love of some worldly creatures alluring us out of the lists wherein we should walk" (*Works*, 10:282).

119. John 17:17.

120. John 17:16. (1) We have a different principle: "Now we have received, not the spirit of the world, but the Spirit which is of God" (1 Cor 2:12). (2) We have a different ruler: "In whom the god of this world hath blinded the minds of them which believe not" (2 Cor 4:4). (3) We have a different course: "In time past ye walked according to the course of this world, according to the prince of the power of the air" (Eph 2:2).

121. John 17:18.

122. John 17:24. "Every verse is sweet," writes Thomas Manton, "but this should not be read without some ravishment and leaping of the heart" (*Works*, 11:89).

123. John 6:40.

124. Job 19:26-27.

125. See John 17:1-5.

way of the cross. That is an acquired glory; it is a glory that is his by virtue of his work (what he does). (2) Christ asked the Father to glorify him with the glory that he possessed before the creation of the world. That is an eternal glory; it is a glory that is his by virtue of his person (who he is). Christ is now glorified—a glorified prophet, who teaches us; a glorified king, who reigns over us; and a glorified priest, who prays for us. In short, he has assumed a position, whereby he exercises his threefold office of prophet, priest, and king, in a greater capacity to do us good. It is for this reason that Wilcox cries, "See Christ your peace"!

## CONCLUSION

It is this constant looking at Christ that makes Wilcox's piety *Christ-centered*. Believing that he is "absolutely nothing" while Christ is "all,"[126] Wilcox endeavors to live with his eyes fixed upon the Rock—Christ. In his own words:

> This will be found religion only, to bottom all upon the everlasting mountains of God's love and grace in Christ, to live continually in the sight of Christ's infinite righteousness and merits (they are sanctifying; without them, the heart is carnal); and in those sights to see the full vileness, yet littleness, of sin, and to see all pardoned; and in those sights to pray, hear, etc., seeing your polluted self, and all your weak performances accepted continually; and in those sights to trample upon all your self-glories, righteousness, and privileges, as abominable, and to be found continually in the righteousness of Christ alone, rejoicing in the ruins of all your own righteousness, the spoiling of all your own excellencies, that Christ alone, as Mediator, may be exalted in his throne.[127]

---

126. Wilcox, *Guide to Eternal Glory*, 15.
127. Ibid., 10.

# 3

# Saving Faith Discovered in Three Heavenly Conferences[1]

## THE FIRST CONFERENCE BETWEEN JESUS AND A PUBLICAN

"IN THE LAST DAY, that great day of the feast, Jesus stood and cried, saying, 'If any man thirst, let him come unto me, and drink'" (John 7:37). "Then drew near unto him all the publicans and sinners for to hear him" (Luke 15:1). And he said to one of them:

---

1. The full title is: *Saving Faith Discovered in Three Heavenly Conferences* in *A Guide to Eternal Glory; or, Brief Directions to All Christians How to Attain Everlasting Salvation; To Which are Added Several Other Excellent Divine Tracts*. In this treatise, there are eleven "tracts" preceded by a preface, signed by Thomas Wilcox. This gives the impression that Wilcox authored all eleven tracts. He did not. Wilcox originally published his sermon, *A Guide to Eternal Glory*, along with a preface. This preface (apart from slight alterations) remains uniform throughout subsequent editions. I have verified this in the 1757, 1767, 1787, and 1797 editions. In 1685, Wilcox's *A Guide to Eternal Glory* was published as part of a collection. His preface was placed at the front of this collection, and this paragraph was inserted: "I have subjoined some other brief tracts, which are intended for the use of honest, plain-hearted Christians, to show them the exceeding willingness of Jesus Christ to help and save poor, humble, repenting and returning sinners; as also his rejecting and casting off proud, self-conceited and self-righteous Pharisees and hypocrites, who having never been sensible of the exceeding sinfulness of sin, do therefore never understand the absolute necessity of a Savior." This preface is signed "G D." In the 1699 edition of this same collection, the preface is maintained with Wilcox's name reaffixed, giving the erroneous impression that this is his collection.

Looking unto Jesus

*Jesus:* Poor publican, what makes thee draw near to me?

*Publican:* Because they say, Lord, that thou art a friend of publicans and sinners (Matt. 11:19).

*Jesus:* So I am, and thou art welcome my beloved friend. Sit down, therefore, with me and my disciples (Matt. 9:10).

*Publican:* Good Master, though I am unworthy to come into thy presence, yet through thy leave I will sit here at thy feet to hear thy gracious words (Mark 7:25; Luke 10:39; John 12:3).

*Jesus:* How knowest thou that my words are gracious?

*Publican:* Lord, I have heard thee say that publicans and harlots shall enter into the kingdom of heaven before the Pharisees, which think themselves far better than us (Matt. 21:31; Luke 18:11–12).

*Jesus:* And what say the Pharisees to that?

*Publican:* They murmur among themselves, and say, "This man receiveth sinners, and eateth with them" (Luke 15:2).

*Jesus:* Didst thou ever hear me preach besides that time?

*Publican:* Yes, once besides, and it was the best and most comfortable sermon that ever I heard.

*Jesus:* Dost thou remember any of it?

*Publican:* Yes. Though I have a bad memory, I remember thou didst say [that] if a man had a hundred sheep, and did lose one of them, he would leave the ninety-nine in the wilderness, and go after that which was lost, until he find it; and when he hath found it, he layeth it on his shoulders, rejoicing; and when he comes home, he calleth together his friends and neighbors, saying unto them, "Rejoice with me; for I have found my sheep which was lost."[2]

*Jesus:* Is that all thou canst remember?

*Publican:* No, I remember somewhat more. Thou didst speak of a woman that had ten pieces of silver. When she had lost one piece, she sought for it till she had found it; then, she called her neighbors together to rejoice with her. Also thou didst speak of a man that had two sons: the one that lived still at home, and was obedient to his father; the other that went away from his father, and spent his father's means among harlots till he

2. See Luke 15:3–6.

## Saving Faith Discovered in Three Heavenly Conferences

came to poverty; and yet, when he returned to his father, his father received him willingly, and gave him great welcome and entertainment.³

*Jesus:* Well done, my friend. Thou hast well remembered; but dost thou know why I speak these comparisons?

*Publican:* No, Sir, I do not well know that.

*Jesus:* It was to comfort and encourage the publicans and great sinners that did hear me, and to silence the Jews that did murmur, because [the publicans] came to hear me, and because I received them.

*Publican:* It is true, Lord. There were many of us there then, but we did not know what thou didst mean by the lost sheep, the lost piece, and the wicked son.

*Jesus:* I did mean thy countrymen and companions (the publicans, harlots, and sinners) that are in a lost condition; because of your sins and wickedness in the eyes of others (as the Pharisees) quite lost, and adjudged to perish forever.

*Publican:* But, Lord, who was it that didst seek for the lost sheep and the lost piece of silver?

*Jesus:* It was I, who am the Savior of sinners, and the Shepherd of the sheep. I am come to seek and to save that which is lost (Matt. 18:11; Luke 19:10).

*Publican:* Lord, I am one of those that are lost. What shall I do to be saved (Acts 16:31)?

*Jesus:* I am the way, and the door. If any man enters in, he shall be saved. Whosoever believeth on me, shall not perish but have everlasting life (John 3:15–16; 10:9; 14:6).

*Publican:* Lord, canst thou save a sinner as I am?

*Jesus:* Yes, I have power to save and power to destroy (Jas. 4:12), but I came not to destroy men's lives, but to save them (Luke 9:56).

*Publican:* And art thou willing, Lord, that I should be saved?

*Jesus:* Yes, I am willing that all should be saved, and come to the knowledge of the truth (1 Tim. 2:5).

*Publican:* But Lord, I am a wicked and sinful man (Luke 5:8).

---

3. See Luke 15:7–32.

*Jesus:* I know, dear son, that thou art so; but I came not to call the righteous, but sinners to repentance (Matt. 9:13).

*Publican:* But Lord, I am not an ordinary, but an extraordinary, sinner.

*Jesus:* Notwithstanding, poor man, hearken for thy comfort. There was a certain creditor which had two debtors: the one owed five hundred pence, and the other fifty. And when they had nothing to pay, he freely forgave them both (Luke 7:41–42).

*Publican:* But Lord, I am a greater sinner than either of them, for I have nothing but sinned all my lifetime.

*Jesus:* What tho', I am come to deliver those that were all their lifetime subject to the bondage of sin (Heb. 2:15).

*Publican:* Lord, be merciful to me, being a sinner, for I think there is not a greater sinner upon earth than I am (Luke 18:13).

*Jesus:* I am merciful, and I will be merciful, and I will pardon thy sins (Jer. 3:12; Heb. 8:12).

*Publican:* Lord, I am such a sinner that I deserve no pardon, for I have wearied thee with my sins.

*Jesus:* Though thou dost not deserve pardon, and though thou hast wearied me with thy sins, yet I will pardon thy iniquities for my own name's sake (Isa. 43:25).

*Publican:* Lord, I think my sins are so great that it is impossible for them to be pardoned.

*Jesus:* Do not think or say so, for all things are possible to him that believeth (Mark 9:23).

*Publican:* But my sins are so red. I think all the water in the sea cannot wash them away.

*Jesus:* Though thy sins be as scarlet, they shall be as white as snow, and though they be red like crimson, they shall be as wool (Isa. 1:18) (if thou wilt turn to me from them), for my blood can cleanse thee from all sin (1 John 1:9).

*Publican:* But Lord, if I should turn to thee from them, yet they are still written down, and thou wilt not blot them out (Jer. 18:23).

*Jesus:* I am he that blotteth out thy transgressions for mine own sake (Isa. 43:25). I have blotted out, as a thick cloud, thy transgressions, and, as a cloud, thy sins. Return unto me; for I have redeemed thee (Isa. 44:22).

*Publican:* But if I should return unto thee, yet when I sin again, thou wilt remember my sins.

*Jesus:* No, I will pardon thee, and thy sins and iniquities will I remember no more (Heb. 10:17).

*Publican:* O Lord, I am the child of wicked parents, and thou hast said [that] thou wilt visit the sins of the father upon the children, to the third and fourth generation.[4]

*Jesus:* If a wicked father begets a son that seeth all his father's sins, which he hath done, and considereth, and doth not such like, that son shall not bear the iniquity of the father (Ezek. 16:3–13; 18:14–17).

*Publican:* But, Lord, were there any wicked parents that had good children?

*Jesus:* Yes, many, as wicked Ahaz had good Hezekiah (2 Kgs. 16:20; 18:3). Idolatrous Amon had zealous Josiah (2 Kgs. 21:21–22; 22:2), and ungodly Saul had godly Jonathan.

*Publican:* Lord, what if I be a bastard, and the child of whoredom?

*Jesus:* That doth not hinder thee neither to be saved, for my servant Jephthah was a bastard (compare Judg. 11:1 with Heb. 11:32); so was my servant Phares, who is reckoned in my own genealogy (compare Gen. 38:18, 29 and Ruth 4:12 with Matt. 1:3).

*Publican:* But Lord, is there not such a Scripture that [says] a bastard shall not enter into thy congregation until the tenth generation?

*Jesus:* Yes, there is such a Scripture (Deut. 23:2), and [it] should make people shun the sin of whoredom, but that doth not exclude men that are born bastards after the flesh, if they be born again of the Spirit, either out of my church on earth (now in the days of the gospel) or yet out of heaven.

*Publican:* But what, Lord, if my father was a bastard?

*Jesus:* Neither doth that hinder, for Zarah, the brother of Phares (who was a bastard), begot my two wise and godly servants Ethan and Heman

---

4. See Exod 34:7.

(compare Gen. 38:30 and 1 Chron. 2:6 with Pss. 88 and 89—the titles of both being "of Heman" and "of Ethan").

*Publican:* O Lord, I am a very old sinner, and have one foot already in the grave, and I fear it is too late for me now to be called.

*Jesus:* No, it is not too late, for I call some at the ninth hour, yea some at the eleventh hour (Matt. 20:6, 9). And I will pour out my Spirit upon old men in these gospel days (Joel 2:28; Acts 2:17).

*Publican:* But Lord, I have committed such great and heinous sins, both by speaking and doing. I am afraid it is in vain for me to seek for mercy.

*Jesus:* Though thou hast spoken and done evil things, as much as thou couldest (Jer. 3:5), yet return unto me, and I will not cause mine anger to fall upon thee, for I am merciful.

*Publican:* How shall I look upon thee, gracious Lord, for I have multiplied sins against thee?

*Jesus:* As thou hast multiplied sins, so will I multiply pardons, if thou wilt return unto me, the Lord (Isa. 55:7).

*Publican:* O, but Lord, I scarce think that any so wicked as myself were saved, for I was an idolater, an adulterer, a thief, a drunkard, and what not that was wicked.

*Jesus:* Such were many of my servants that are now in heaven, but I according to my own kindness and pity to them, saved them by washing, sanctifying, and justifying them by my own name, blood, and Spirit (1 Cor. 6:9–11; Titus 3:3–7).

*Publican:* O, but merciful Savior, I was a ringleader of others into sin, and I enticed, and drew many into wickedness, and therefore my case is far worse than others.

*Jesus:* As thou wast a ringleader and enticer of others into sin, so I can make thee a guide and leader of others into, and in the way of, righteousness, as I made thy countryman, Levi, and others.[5]

*Publican:* But that which makes me fear most is because I was a blasphemer, reviler, and persecutor of thy people, yea many of thy saints did I shut up in prison.

---

5. See Matt 9:9–10.

*Jesus:* Yet thou shalt have mercy, because thou didst it ignorantly through unbelief (1 Tim. 1:13).

*Publican:* But Lord, I find my heart is so hardened through the deceitfulness and custom of sin that I cannot hope it will ever be otherwise.

*Jesus:* I can and will take away the stony heart out of thy flesh, and I will give thee a heart of flesh (Ezek. 36:26).

*Publican:* Lord, wilt thou do all for me?

*Jesus:* I must do all for thee, for without me thou canst do nothing (John 15:5; Phil. 2:13).

*Publican:* Lord, what then shall I do?

*Jesus:* Before I teach thee what thou must do, I will first show thee what I have done and suffered for thee.

*Publican:* Good Master, I desire to know that.

*Jesus:* (1) I left my own glory, and came into the world to save thee, and such sinners as thou art (John 17:5; 1 Tim. 1:15). (2) Though I was the only Son of my Father, and in his own form, and equal to him, yet I took upon me the form of a servant, for thee and thy brethren's sake (John 1:14; Phil. 2:6-8). (3) Though I was Heir of all things, and Possessor of heaven and earth, yet I became poor and hungry, that thou mightest be made rich (Gen. 14:19; 2 Cor. 8:9; Heb. 1:2). (4) Though I deserved honor and glory, yet I was reviled, threatened, and persecuted by my own creatures, and all for my good will to thee (Heb. 2:9; 1 Pet. 2:23). (5) Though I had no sin, yet I was made sin that thou, poor sinner, mightest escape sin (2 Cor. 1:21; 1 Pet. 1:19; 2:22). (6) Though I was a Law-giver and Law-maker (Isa. 3:13; 33:22), yet I became under the curse of my own Law, that I might redeem thee from that curse. (7) [Though] I had power over my own life, and no man could take it from me, yet I laid it down for thee, that thou mightest have life (John 10:18; Rom. 5:6, 9; 1 John 3:16). (8) Though I was my Father's delight, and an object of his love from everlasting, yet I became an object of his wrath, for my love to thee (Prov. 8:30; Pss. 88:1; 102:10). (9) When thou wast an enemy, and a stranger to God, my Father, I made peace between him and thee, and reconciled thee to him by my death and sufferings (Rom. 5:10; Col. 1:20-21; Eph. 2:12-13). (10) When thou wast a slave to the devil (2 Tim. 2:26), and a fire-brand of hell (Amos 4:11), I did rescue thee from the power of the one (Heb. 2:14), and redeem thee from the plague and punishment of the other (1 Thess. 1:10).

*Publican:* O Lord, I did not deserve any of this from thee.

*Jesus:* True, thou didst not deserve it, but yet I did it freely and out of love to thee (Rom. 3:24; Eph. 5:2).

*Publican:* Are all my sins, Lord, satisfied for, and done away, by thy death?

*Jesus:* Yes, they are perfectly satisfied for, and absolutely done away out of my Father's sight, never to be imputed again to thee (2 Cor. 5:19).

*Publican:* And is there nothing now in the way that hinders me to be saved?

*Jesus:* No, there is nothing, for I have taken all things out of the way, that hindered thee to be saved (Col. 2:14).

*Publican:* And am I to do nothing to be saved?

*Jesus:* Nothing at all towards thy own salvation, for I have bought thee from death, and purchased thee life and salvation (1 Cor. 6:20; Eph. 1:14; 1 Pet. 1:18).

*Publican:* Shall I then be saved, Lord?

*Jesus:* Yes, if thou wilt believe, and trust wholly and only upon me, and upon my righteousness and merits, thou shalt be saved (John 3:36; Rom. 9:33; 10:9, 11).

*Publican:* Lord, I would believe, but I partly am afraid to believe; and partly I am so weak I cannot believe.

*Jesus:* Thou poor fearful heart, fear not, but be strong (Isa. 34:5). But tell me why thou art afraid?

*Publican:* Lest I should presume, or lest I should believe, and have no ground for my faith.

*Jesus:* It is not presumption for thee to do what I command thee, but it is obedience, and is not my word of promise a sufficient ground for thy faith (John 5:24; 1 John 3:23)?

*Publican:* Dost thou then, Lord, command me to believe?

*Jesus:* Yes. Fear not, believe on me, and thou shalt be saved (Luke 8:50; Acts 16:31).

*Publican:* But, Lord, though thou commandest me, yet I have no power to believe.

*Jesus:* I will write my laws in thy heart (Heb. 8:10), and will enable and give thee power to believe (Matt. 12:21).

*Publican:* Lord, if thou wilt also give me power to believe, I will acknowledge I am nothing, but what I am in thee, and that I have nothing, but what I have received from thee.

*Jesus:* Dost thou now believe?

*Publican:* O yes, now, Lord, I believe (John 9:38).

*Jesus:* This is the work and gift of God that thou dost believe; for flesh and blood hath not wrought this in thee (John 6:29; Eph. 2:8).

*Publican:* O Lord, I do acknowledge it to be thy work, but I am afraid I shall lose this faith again.

*Jesus:* I, that am the Author of thy faith, will also finish it (Heb. 12:2). Be, therefore, of good cheer, for thou art one of my Father's children, and of my saints, and my spirit shall abide in thee forever (John 1:12; 4:14; 7:38–39).

*Publican:* Lord, I have sinned against thy Father, and against thee, and I am unworthy to be called either his son or thy servant (Luke 15:21).

*Jesus:* Son, thy sins are forgiven thee; sin no more (Luke 5:23; John 8:11).

*Publican:* Lord, I am afraid I shall sin again, though I desire and resolve never to do it; but what, Lord, if I should sin against my will?

*Jesus:* Thou canst not sin willingly and willfully, for my seed of grace will remain in thee (1 John 3:9), and if thou sinnest through weakness and frailty, I will be an Advocate, and a propitiation for thy sins (1 John 2:1–2, 12).

*Publican:* Is it thy will, Lord, that I should have forgiveness of my sins, and doubt no more?

*Jesus:* Yes, surely, for these things have I spoken that thou shouldest have a full assurance, and doubt no more.

*Publican:* But what if Satan, when he sees me sin, shall tempt me to doubt again?

*Jesus:* Say unto him that I am faithful and just to forgive thee thy sins, and that my blood cleanseth thee from all sin (1 John 1:7).

*Publican:* But Lord, wilt thou not have me to confess my sins?

Looking unto Jesus

*Jesus:* Yes, I will have thee to confess them, and forsake them (Prov. 28:13; 1 John 1:9).

*Publican:* But Lord, is it thy mind that I should always be sorrowful?

*Jesus:* No, but it is thy mind, rather that thou shouldest always rejoice, and have strong consolation (Phil. 4:4; Heb. 6:18).

*Publican:* O Lord, I cannot choose but cry and mourn, and be ashamed, and hate myself for all my former wickedness and ungodliness (Ezek. 16:61).

*Jesus:* Thou mayest do that, and yet hold fast thy confidence, for the spirit of mourning, and the spirit of grace and adoption, may be in thy heart at once, and the one not destroy the other (Zech. 12:10).

*Publican:* Lord, how is that?

*Jesus:* Thou mayest mourn at the sight of thy sins, as they were committed against me, and for thy denying, selling and crucifying me, and yet thou mayest believe (because I have said so) that they are all pardoned. As Joseph's brothers cried and complained for their guiltiness in selling him, yet they were glad that he was alive, and could help them in their distress (Gen. 42:21–22).

*Publican:* Now Lord, thou hast taught me what I should do in respect of myself, but now, Lord, I would do something for thee.

*Jesus:* Come, then, and follow me (Matt. 9:9).

And he arose and followed him.

## THE SECOND CONFERENCE BETWEEN JESUS AND A PHARISEE

Then one of the Pharisees came to him, and asked him, "What shall we do, that we might work the works of God?" (John 6:28).

*Jesus:* This is the work of God, that thou believest in him whom he hath sent (John 6:29).

*Pharisee:* But, Master, what good thing shall I do, that I may have eternal life? (Matt. 19:16).

*Jesus:* If thou wilt be saved by doing, then keep the Ten Commandments.

*Pharisee:* I have kept them all from my youth (Matt. 19:20).

*Jesus:* Then, thou art no sinner.

*Pharisee:* Yes, we are all sinners; but I thank God that I am not as other men are, extortionists, unjust, adulterers, or even as this publican (Luke 18:11).

*Jesus:* Why? What dost thou more than this publican?

*Pharisee:* I fast twice in the week and give tithes of all that I possess, and concerning the Law, I live blameless (Luke 18:12; Phil. 3:6).

*Jesus:* Hast thou never read that they, which followed after the Law of righteousness, have not attained to the Law of righteousness (Rom. 9:31)?

*Pharisee:* No, I never observed that, but I remember another text, where God saith, "I gave them my statutes, and showed them my judgments, which if a man do, he shall even live in them" (Ezek. 20:11).

*Jesus:* Dost thou think to go to heaven by doing?

*Pharisee:* Not by doing only, but by doing good and departing evil.

*Jesus:* But doth not the Law say, "Cursed is he that observeth not all things that are written in the words of the Law to do them" (Deut. 27:26).

*Pharisee:* Yes, that is whosoever breaks the Law is accursed unless he repents for it.

*Jesus:* The Law doth not say that unless men repent for breaking it they are accursed, but it says absolutely that they are accursed (Gal. 3:10); and I say, whosoever keepeth the whole Law, and yet offendeth in one point, he is guilty of all (Matt. 5:19; Jas. 2:10).

*Pharisee:* I say so too, that except men keep the Law of Moses they cannot be saved (Acts 15:1, 24); and whosoever know not and keep not the Law, they are accursed (John 7:49).

*Jesus:* Dost thou know the Law?

*Pharisee:* Yes, I know the Law, for I am instructed daily out of the Law, by our doctors of the Law and holy priests (Zeph. 3:4).

*Jesus:* The priests have done violence to the Law, and they that handle the Law know not the Lord (Jer. 3:8).

*Pharisee:* Jehovah hath said that the Law shall not perish from the priest, for the priest's lips is to keep knowledge, and we are to seek the Law at his mouth (Jer. 18:18; Mal. 2:7).

Looking unto Jesus

*Jesus:* God hath said also that the Law shall perish from the priest, and that they shall not every man teach his neighbor any more, for all will know the Lord from the least to the greatest (Jer. 31:34).

*Pharisee:* I perceive thou goest about to destroy the Law.

*Jesus:* Think not so, for I am not come to destroy the Law, but to fulfill it (Matt. 5:17; Luke 16:17).

*Pharisee:* Aye Sir, I like that, that we should fulfill the Law, that we should perform it.

*Jesus:* Yes, Moses gave you the Law, but none of you keep it (John 7:19), but you have been partial in the Law (Mal. 2:9). Ye pay tithe of mint and anise and cummin, and have omitted the weightier matters of the law, judgment, mercy, and faith (Matt. 23:23).

*Pharisee:* It is true, we may come short in some things, but he that keepeth the Law happy is he.

*Jesus:* Thou that restest in the Law, and makest thy boast of the Law (Rom. 2:17, 23), through breaking the Law thou dost dishonor God, and causest many to stumble at the Law (Mal. 2:8). Verily, I say unto thee, thou shalt be judged by the Law (Rom. 2:12).

*Pharisee:* No, I hope rather to be justified than to be judged by the Law.

*Jesus:* Verily, verily, I say unto thee, by the deeds of the Law, there shall be no flesh justified in God's sight (Rom. 3:20; Gal. 3:11).

*Pharisee:* How then shall I be justified?

*Jesus:* The righteousness of God without the Law is manifest, being witnessed by the Law and the Prophets (Rom. 3:21).

*Pharisee:* What righteousness is that?

*Jesus:* Not a man's own righteousness (Phil. 3:9), which is called the righteousness of the Law (Rom. 2:26), but the righteousness which is of God by faith (Rom. 4:13).

*Pharisee:* What difference is there between the righteousness of the Law, and the righteousness of faith?

*Jesus:* Moses describeth the righteousness of the Law thus, that the man which doth those things which the Law requireth shall live by them; but the righteousness of faith saith, "whosoever believeth on him shall not be ashamed" (Rom. 10:5–6, 11).

*Pharisee:* How can men be saved by believing in thee, for thou art but one?

*Jesus:* As by one man's offence death reigned (Rom. 5:9), by one much more, they which receive abundance of grace and of the gifts of righteousness, shall reign in life by me, who am the Son of righteousness (Mal. 4:2), and made by God my Father to be righteousness unto men (1 Cor. 1:30).

*Pharisee:* Thou bearest record of thyself (John 8:13).

*Jesus:* Though I bear record of myself, yet my record is true (John 8:14). My Father also beareth witness of me, and this is his witness, that he hath given life, and this life is in me, his Son (1 John 5:11).

*Pharisee:* But what sayest thou? How was our father, Abraham, and his seed, who lived before thee, justified and saved?

*Jesus:* Your father Abraham rejoiced to see my day, and he saw it, and was glad (Jn. 8:56), for I was before Abraham, and he and his spiritual seed were justified and saved by faith in me (Rom. 4:3, 11, 13, 16; Gal. 3:14, 18, 20).

*Pharisee:* But was not Abraham justified by works?

*Jesus:* If Abraham were justified by works, he hath whereof to glory, but not before God; for what saith the Scripture? "Abraham believed God, and it was counted unto him for righteousness" (Rom. 4:3).

*Pharisee:* If I be not justified by my good works, to what end should I perform them?

*Jesus:* Though thy good works cannot justify thee before God, yet they may glorify God, and be profitable unto men (Matt. 5:16; Titus 3:8).

*Pharisee:* Well then, I am glad my good works are good for something.

*Jesus:* Yes, thy good works would be good for something if thy faith (like Abraham's) did work with thy works (Jas. 2:22), but thou dost not believe, and all thy works thou dost to be seen of men (Matt. 23:5).

*Pharisee:* No, I do not my good works to be seen of men, but to please God.

*Jesus:* I tell thee that without faith it is impossible to please God (Heb. 11:6).

*Pharisee:* But God hath said that, if a man doeth well, he shall be accepted.[6]

---

6. See Gen 4:7.

*Jesus:* It is not for their well-doing that men are accepted with my Father, but they are made acceptable in me, and their works are accepted for my sake (Eph. 1:6; 1 Pet. 2:6).

*Pharisee:* But am I no nearer heaven, that perform good works, than this sinful and ungodly publican?

*Jesus:* Thou hypocrite that justifiest thyself, and judgest another. I tell thee that publicans and harlots shall enter into the kingdom of heaven before such as thou art (Matt. 7:5; 21:31).

*Pharisee:* O, untrue and false doctrine, to say that those cursed men who know not the Law should be saved before us, who are the children of Abraham (John 7:49; 8:33).

*Jesus:* Thou blind and self-conceited Pharisee, understandest thou not the Scripture? "'I will have mercy and not sacrifice': for I am not come to call the righteous, but sinners to repentance" (Matt. 9:13). And I say unto thee, unless thou dost believe in me, thou art not the child of Abraham (Gal. 3:26).

*Pharisee:* I believe in the God of Abraham, the God of Isaac, and the God of Jacob, whose child and servant I am.

*Jesus:* If thou didst believe in God, thou wouldst also believe in me, but thou art the child of the devil, and in bondage to this day (John 8:44; Gal. 4:25).

*Pharisee:* How am I in bondage?

*Jesus:* Thou art under the curse of the Law, and under the power of sin and Satan; and canst never be made free unless I make thee free (John 8:34–36).

*Pharisee:* How dost thou free men?

*Jesus:* By my death and sufferings I satisfy the Law (Gal. 3:13); by the power of my resurrection, I overcome death (1 Cor. 15:55–57); and by my Spirit, I cast out Satan and subdue sin (Matt. 12:28; Rom. 8:2).

*Pharisee:* Sir, I hope to be freed another way, to wit, by my sacrifices, prayers, and good works.

*Jesus:* Thy sacrifices and thy prayers are an abomination unto me (Prov. 15:8; 28:9; Isa. 66:3), and thy works are not found perfect before God (Rev. 3:2).

*Pharisee:* What, dost thou think to beat me off from my long prayers and good works? I hope by these, together with my fasting and mourning, to lay a sure and happy foundation for my soul forever.

*Jesus:* Thou worker of iniquity, that dost practice hypocrisy (Isa. 32:6). I tell thee thy prayers are sin (Ps. 109:7), thy works are done to be seen of man. Thou also fastest for strife (Isa. 58:4–5), and thy mourning is but hypocritical. Therefore, instead of laying a sure and happy foundation, thou heapest up wrath to thyself against the day of wrath (Job 36:13).

*Pharisee:* Sir, I am not a hypocrite, but a true child of God, and I hope I shall be saved, for I know most good men take me for a godly and righteous man.

*Jesus:* Though thou dost outwardly appear righteous unto men (Matt. 23:28), yet within thou art full of hypocrisy and iniquity. Thou seed of the serpent, thy hope shall perish, for thou canst not escape the damnation of hell (Job 8:13).[7]

*Pharisee:* I do not fear what thou sayest, for I am better persuaded of myself.

*Jesus:* Though thy seared conscience, and hardened heart, hinders thee yet from fearing, yet fear, terror and trembling shall surprise and fill thy spirit (Isa. 33:14), and thou shalt roar in flames of fire, and in everlasting burnings (Deut. 32:22; Mark 9:43–44, 46; Luke 3:17).

*Pharisee:* I have joy and comfort in my spirit often from my performances, and I know that God will hear my prayers that I make publicly and privately unto him.

*Jesus:* Thou painted sepulcher, hast thou not read that the joy of a hypocrite is but for a moment (Job 20:5), and that a hypocrite shall not come before God (Job 13:16)? And dost not thou restrain prayer before God (Job 15:4). And when thou prayest, dost thou not do it publicly to be seen of men (Matt. 6:5)?

*Pharisee:* I pray in private also.

*Jesus:* Then it is either when some punishment is upon thee, or else to quiet thy carnal conscience (Isa. 26:16).

*Pharisee:* Master, why dost thou reproach me in saying this?

---

7. Powell includes another reference, but it is illegible.—ed.

*Jesus:* Thou dissembler that seekest honor of men (John 5:44), and not the honor which cometh from God. Thou art to expect nothing but shame and everlasting contempt (Dan. 12:2).

*Pharisee:* Sir, thou judgest rashly.

*Jesus:* No, as I hear I judge, and my judgment is just and true (John 5:30; 8:16, 26).

*Pharisee:* How knowest thou that I am what thou so judgest?

*Jesus:* I am he that searcheth the reins and hearts; and I will give unto every one of you according to your works (Rev. 2:23).

*Pharisee:* When thou judgest the world, what difference wilt thou make between us that serve God and the heathens that served him not?

*Jesus:* The difference will be this, that your condemnation will be greater (Matt. 23:14), because, though ye know God, yet ye served him selfishly and hypocritically (Isa. 57:4; Matt. 15:9; Mark 12:40; Luke 20:47).

*Pharisee:* Good Master, I would escape this condemnation, for I believe it will be great, and thy words begin to terrify me already.

*Jesus:* I have told thee already that there is no other way for thee to escape it, but only by me, yet thou dost not believe in me (John 10:25).

*Pharisee:* How wilt thou have me believe in thee?

*Jesus:* First, I will have thee see thyself to be the greatest and vilest of sinners (1 Tim. 1:15), and then see all thy own righteousness, services, and performances, to be as filthy and menstrual rags (Isa. 64:6). And after thou hast denied and abhorred thyself (Ezek. 36:31), then cry out, "Master, save me, or else I perish," for the whole need not a physician, but those that are sick (Matt. 9:12).

*Pharisee:* I do see myself a sinner, and am sorry for my sins. And doth not God say that whosoever confesseth and forsaketh his sins shall find mercy?

*Jesus:* I say unto thee, thou lukewarm professor, except thou eatest my flesh and drinkest my blood, and submittest unto my righteousness, thou canst not be saved (John 6:53–54).

*Pharisee:* Well then, if I cannot be saved by my own works and righteousness, Master, let me be beholding to thee to save me.

*Jesus:* Hast thou not read that salvation belongeth only to the Lord (Ps. 3:8), and that men are saved by grace without the works of the Law? Why then dost thou so lightly esteem the Rock of thy salvation (Deut. 32:15) by seeking to be justified and saved (as it were) by thy own works (Rom. 9:32)? I tell thee again, thou must deny thy own righteousness wholly, and look to be found in my righteousness only, else thou canst not be saved (Phil. 3:9).

*Pharisee:* Indeed, Master, thou makest the way to heaven very hard.

*Jesus:* It is so hard that many shall seek to enter in, and shall not be able (Luke 13:24).

*Pharisee:* If it be as thou sayest, I am afraid many of our best Scribes and Pharisees will come short of heaven.

*Jesus:* Thou mayest be sure of that, for verily I say unto thee that except thy righteousness exceed the righteousness of the Scribes and Pharisees, thou shalt in no case enter into the kingdom of heaven (Matt. 5:20).

*Pharisee:* But, Master, there be some that do great works in thy name. Shall not all such be saved?

*Jesus:* No, for many will say unto me hereafter, "Lord, Lord, have we not prophesied in thy name? and in thy name have cast out devils? and in thy name done many wonderful works?" And then will I profess unto them, "I never knew you: depart from me, ye that work iniquity" (Matt. 7:22–23).

*Pharisee:* But why should not such rather be saved than cast away?

*Jesus:* Because they (as thou dost) do all those things to be seen of men, and to gain honor unto themselves, and so build their salvation upon this false foundation, as the foolish builder built his house upon the sand, which in time of flood and wind could not stand, but fell (Matt. 7:26–27).

*Pharisee:* I see thou dost reject me. I thought to be one of thy disciples, and to follow thee.

*Jesus:* No. I do not reject thee, but am very willing to receive thee; but first consider what thou dost, and what it will cost thee, if thou wilt be my disciples and follow me.

*Pharisee:* What will it cost me, Master?

*Jesus:* Thou must hate thy father, and mother, and wife, and children, and brothers, and sisters, and thy own life also; yea, thou must go, and sell all that thou hast and take up thy cross daily and follow me, else thou canst not be my disciple (Luke 14:26–27).

*Pharisee:* This is a hard saying, who can bear it (John 6:60, 66)?

And he went away sorrowful, and followed him no more (Matt. 19:22).

## THE THIRD CONFERENCE BETWEEN JESUS AND A DOUBTING CHRISTIAN

*Jesus:* Come unto me, all ye that labor and are heavy laden, and I will give you rest (Matt. 11:28).

*Christian:* O Lord, I am a poor, heavy laden sinner that would come unto thee, but cannot come.

*Jesus:* It is true, O soul, no man can come unto me, except the Father which hath sent me draw him (John 6:44).

*Christian:* How then shall I come unto thee?

*Jesus:* I and my Father are one (John 10:30), and we give power to the faint, and to them that have no might, we add strength (Isa. 40:29).

*Christian:* Lord, I am altogether without strength; therefore, draw me unto thee, and I will come.

*Jesus:* I will draw thee unto me with the cords of a man, with bands of love (Hos. 11:4), and with loving kindness (Jer. 31:3; John 12:31).

*Christian:* But Lord, now I look upon myself. I feel I am unworthy to come unto thee; yea, unworthy of the least of thy mercies.

*Jesus:* So said my servants John the Baptist (Matt. 3:14), and Jacob (Gen. 32:10), and others (Matt. 8:8; Luke 7:7), yet do not judge thyself (as the Jews did) unworthy of eternal life (Acts 13:46).

*Christian:* If such men as John the Baptist and Jacob did judge themselves unworthy; how many thousand times more unworthy am I, a wretched and wicked sinner?

*Jesus:* It is true neither they nor thou could be worthy of yourselves, but yet I am willing to account you worthy (Luke 20:35; 21:36; Rev. 3:4).

*Christian:* But Lord, if there were anything that were good in me, it might a little encourage me to come unto thee, but I find nothing but evil in me.

*Jesus:* Dost thou know that without me thou canst do nothing (John 15:5), and that a man can receive nothing except it be given him from heaven (John 3:27)? Why then dost thou stay away from me who must work all thy works in thee (Isa. 26:12)? And because thou seest nothing but evil in thee, thou shouldest the rather come unto me, who am the fountain wherein thy unclean soul must be washed (Zech 13:1). Unless I wash thee, thou canst not be clean, nor have any part in me (Ezek. 36:25; John 13:8).

*Christian:* True, Lord, thou art the fountain and well spring of life, and it is thy blood (and nothing else) that can wash away my sins; but how can I come near to thee, who am so wicked, that for ought I know, have counted thy blood an unholy thing (Heb. 10:29).

*Jesus:* Thou poor, dear and doubting soul, what if thou hadst had a hand in crucifying me (as the Jews had), yet cannot I forgive thee, as I did many of them (Acts 2:36, 41)? But thou hast not counted my blood an unholy thing, for thou desirest to have thy sins washed away by it.

*Christian:* What the Jews did they did ignorantly; but I have sinned against knowledge, which makes my sins worse than theirs.

*Jesus:* If thou hast sinned against knowledge, yet thou hast not sinned so, but that thou mayest be forgiven; for my dear disciple Peter sinned against knowledge, when he denied with an oath that he knew me not (Matt. 26:72).

*Christian:* O, but yet my sins are worse than his, for his sin was but one sin, and that a sudden and short sin; but I have sinned many sins and continued long in them.

*Jesus:* So did my beloved servant David (who was a man according to my own heart) commit several sins together, as murder, whoredom, etc., and continued a while too in his sins.

*Christian:* O, but Lord, those servants of thine, though they sinned against thee, yet they expressed a great deal of sense of their sins, and sorrow for them; but I can neither be sensible of, nor sorrowful for, mine.

*Jesus:* O sweet soul, thou mistakest and forgettest thyself, for thou dost often confess thy sins before me with sense, shame, and sorrow.

And I hear thee daily bemoaning and complaining and saying, "I have sinned against the Lord. Woe is me for I am undone" (Job 7:20; Ps. 51:4; Lam. 5:16).

*Christian:* O good Lord, it is not without a cause that I cry, "Woe is me I am undone," for I think there is no soul in such a dangerous and desperate condition as mine is in.

*Jesus:* Why dost thou think and say so?

*Christian:* Because I have sinned that unpardonable sin against thy Spirit.

*Jesus:* O, thou poor and precious soul, thou dost but think so; but tell me how canst thou sin that sin against my Spirit, and yet pray for more of my Spirit, and so much prize my Spirit as thou dost?

*Christian:* O Lord, I have often grieved and quenched thy Spirit, and is not this to commit the unpardonable sin?

*Jesus:* My own dear and loving children may and do sometimes grieve my Spirit by sinning, and quench the gracious motions of it, and yet do not sin that unpardonable sin (Eph. 4:30; 1 Thess. 5:19).[8]

*Christian:* O, but I can think no less but that I have committed that sin, for I have had hard, cruel, and desperate thoughts in my heart against the Holy Spirit.

*Jesus:* Though, my child, thou hast had such thoughts in thy heart, yet thou hast not spoken evil of my Spirit (as the Jews did) which is the sin of blasphemy, and that unpardonable sin (Matt. 12:24–31; Mark 3:22–30).

*Christian:* Lord, I am not sure but that I have spoken evil words of thy Spirit, for I know I have many times uttered vile, bitter, and cursed words.

*Jesus:* Notwithstanding, thou didst through the violence of thy temptations, and in the bitterness of thy soul, speak such words, as my servants Job (Job 3:10; 10:18; 23:15–16), David (Pss. 31:22; 116:11), Jeremiah (Jer. 20:14), Jonah (Jonah 4:3, 9), and Peter (Matt. 26:27, 74) did, yet thou hast not done despitefully (nor sinned maliciously and willfully) against my Spirit of grace as reprobates do (Heb. 10:29).

*Christian:* O, I have been and still am very willful, and have often sinned willfully, and thou sayest in thy word that if any sin willfully after they

---

8. Powell includes another reference, but it is illegible.—ed.

## Saving Faith Discovered in Three Heavenly Conferences

receive the knowledge of the truth, there remaineth no more sacrifice for sins (Heb. 10:26).

*Jesus:* Thou dear soul, have not I heard thee often in prayer complaining of, and bewailing, thy sins, and begging earnestly for power against them? Therefore, it is rather against thy will, than willfully, that thou dost sin.

*Christian:* O, but I find sin in power in my soul, which if I were a saint, it would not be so.

*Jesus:* My servant Paul found sin so strong in him that he confessed he was carnal, and sold under sin, and that he found a law in his members, warring against the law of his mind, and bringing him into captivity to the law of sin (Rom. 7:23).

*Christian:* O, but neither Paul, nor any other saint, hath sinned presumptuously as I have done.

*Jesus:* My servant David prayed that he might be kept from presumptuous sins, for he was subject thereunto, and so are the best of my saints.

*Christian:* But Lord, I have rebelled against thee.

*Jesus:* So did my servants of old (Isa. 1:2; 63:20),[9] but I have received gifts for the rebellious (Ps. 68:18), and to me belong mercies and forgiveness, though thou hast rebelled against me (Dan. 9:9).

*Christian:* O, but my rebellion is the worst rebellion of all, for I have rebelled against the light; I have professed thee, and yet I have belied thee, and made a hypocritical profession; I seemed like Judas, to be thy friend, while in my heart I did not love thee.

*Jesus:* The house of Israel and the house of Judah dealt treacherously against me (Jer. 5:11–12, 18), the Lord, and belied me, and Ephraim, my dear son, compassed me about with lies (Hos. 11:12), yet was I gracious to them (Jer. 23:6; 31:20).

*Christian:* But, Lord, Ephraim was never so wicked as I am, and guilty of such lukewarmness, hypocrisy, and backsliding, as I am guilty of.

*Jesus:* Yes, Ephraim was a cake not turned. And Ephraim fed upon wind and provoked me to anger most bitterly, yet my bowels still worked toward Ephraim, that I could not destroy him (Hos. 8:8; 11:8; 12:1, 14).

---

9. Isa 63:20 does not exist.—ed.

*Christian:* But I increased in sin, and the more mercies received, the more my heart was exalted.

*Jesus:* Even so did Ephraim sin more and more, according as he was filled, so his heart was exalted (Hos. 13:2, 6).

*Christian:* But Lord, what didst thou do to Ephraim?

*Jesus:* I drew them with the cords of a man, and with bonds of love, and I was as the dew unto them (Hos. 11:4; 14:5).

*Christian:* O, but I have forsaken the Lord, and back-slided from thee.

*Jesus:* So did Israel and Judah (Jer. 2:13; 3:6; 4:16).

*Christian:* But Lord, I find that my heart is bent to continual back-sliding, yea, my back-slidings are increased.

*Jesus:* So were they (Jer. 5:6; Hos 11:7), yet I healed their back-slidings; so will I heal thine also (Jer. 3:14, 22; Hos. 14:4).

*Christian:* But I have fallen into gross sins that have dishonored thee, and caused thine enemies to blaspheme.

*Jesus:* So did my servant David (2 Sam. 12:14) and others of my saints.

*Christian:* But then he did mourn and repent greatly for his sins, but I cannot do so, for I find my heart hard as an adamant.

*Jesus:* So my people Israel's hearts formerly were as hard as a rock, adamant and flint (Jer. 5:3; Ezek. 3:9).

*Christian:* O, but I have been long (yea ever) troubled with this hardness of heart.

*Jesus:* What tho', yet I am exalted to give repentance unto you (Acts 5:31).

*Christian:* O, but I do not find I am sensible enough of my sin, for if I were, I should mourn and be ashamed for all the wickedness, which I have committed against thee.

*Jesus:* When thou dost see me, whom thou hast pierced (Rev. 1:7), and when thou seest that I am pacified toward thee, then thou shalt mourn, loathe thyself and be ashamed, for all thy sins and abominations, which thou hast committed against me (Ezek. 6:9; 16:63).

*Christian:* But Lord, I am a very great sinner, and I would fain see the nature and number of my sins, that I might truly repent me of them, and be humbled for them.

*Jesus:* If thou seest all thy sins, with their nature, number and aggravation, thou canst never look upon them but with despair as Cain (Gen. 4:13) and Judas (Matt. 27:3-5). And it is not so much the sight of sin, as the sight of my love, grace, goodness, and glory, that will lead thee to repentance, and humble thee for thy sins (Zech. 12:10; Ps. 6:5; Luke 7:42, 47; Rom. 2:4).

*Christian:* O Lord, I know I am as wicked a sinner, and as ungodly a wretch, as ever lived; but though I know this, yet methinks I am not broken with the sense thereof, I cannot weep nor shed tears for my sins. O no! I go many times to prayer, and to hear sermons, and there is no more working nor relenting upon my soul than if I were a dead stock or stone.

*Jesus:* O, my dear soul, do not thou belie thyself, for I have heard many a sorrowful sigh coming from thy heart, and I have seen many a tear drop from thine eyes (Ps. 34:17; Ezek. 9:4); and I will yet pour out more of the Spirit of mourning upon thee (Zech. 12:10-12). But what if thou didst not find these things in thyself, yet I have offered up strong cries and tears unto my Father for thee (Heb. 5:7).

*Christian:* O Lord, that I had but faith to believe that for myself.

*Jesus:* Have faith in me, and be not faithless but believing (Mark 11:13;[10] John 20:27).

*Christian:* Lord, I find so much atheism and unbelief in my heart that I have oftentimes questionings in myself concerning God and concerning the Scriptures and [the] word of God.

*Jesus:* These are the temptations and suggestions of Satan, and my own disciples were and are troubled with them (Luke 24:25).

*Christian:* O Lord, I am troubled with a thousand temptations.

*Jesus:* Yet fear not, my loving and dear child, though thou hast divers temptations (Jas. 1:2), for it is that which my best saints have had, and I will not suffer thee to be tempted above what thou art able (1 Cor. 10:13), but I will succor thee in thy temptations (Heb. 2:18), and I will make a way that thou wilt escape and be delivered out of temptations (2 Pet. 2:9).

---

10. Mark 11:22-23?—ed.

*Christian*: But I think no saint hath such temptations as mine, for sometimes I am tempted to kill myself, and sometimes to kill others, insomuch that I cannot look upon any weapon, waters, or the like, but I am ready to make myself away therewith.

*Jesus*: Satan tempted me to cast myself off the pinnacle of the temple (Matt. 4:5), and he also tempted many of my dear children to destroy themselves; but do not thou hearken to the accuser, for he doth accuse thee to me and me to thee (Rev. 12:10), but rather say unto him, "Satan it is written [that] my Lord Jesus hath overcome thee, and I hope through his blood, and through his might and spirit to overcome thee likewise." Say also, "My God hath commanded me not to kill another (Ex. 20:13), nor to do hurt or violence to myself (Acts 16:28); therefore, get thee behind me, thou liar, murderer, and enemy, for I will put my trust in Christ, though he kill me (Job 13:15), and I will endeavor to live to serve him, though he should afterwards damn me."

*Christian*: O, but this doth much trouble me, that I do not find any love in my heart to thee.

*Jesus*: What though thou dost not, yet I will circumcise thy heart and thou shalt love me; and when thou apprehendest my love to thee, thou wilt love me again (Deut. 30:6; 1 John 4:19).

*Christian*: I have sinned, Lord, against thy mercies, and abused thy love, yea loved my sins more than thee; therefore, I cannot think that ever thou wilt look upon me with any love or delight.

*Jesus*: So did my servant David (2 Sam. 12:8–9) and my people Israel (Hos. 2:5), yet as I loved them, so will I love thee freely, and betroth thee to me in loving kindness and mercy (Hos. 14:4).

*Christian*: But Lord, I have not only sinned against thy mercies, but against thy corrections and chastisements also.

*Jesus*: So did my people Israel formerly, for when I smote them, they went on forwardly in the way of their evil hearts, but I led them, and restored comforts to them (Isa. 57:17–18).

*Christian*: Aye, but my condition is worse than all that, for I have been long under the means of grace, and yet I am altogether fruitless, and like the barren fig-tree.

*Jesus:* Thou troubled soul, in me is thy fruit found, and I will purge thee, and thou wilt bring forth fruit abundantly (John 15:4), for they that are planted in my house shall flourish and be fat, and [be] like a green olive tree (Ps. 92:12-14).

*Christian:* Aye Lord, it is true if I were a branch in thee, and a true member of thy house, then I could believe these promises of thine; alas I am neither of both, but separated from thee and thy people.

*Jesus:* Do not say that thou art none of mine, for I have bought thee with my blood, and do not speak that thou art separated from my people, for I will give thee in my house, and within my walls, a place and a name of sons and daughters (Isa. 56:3, 5).

*Christian:* Surely, if I were not an outcast and a reprobate, I should not be thus, as I am, in a wilderness condition.

*Jesus:* Israel was counted as an outcast, and she cried out, yet I was then a God to her, and she a people to me (Jer. 30:16, 17, 22).

*Christian:* O, if I were but one of thine, I should then count myself the happiest in all the world.

*Jesus:* Fear not my spouse, for I am thy husband and thy father.

*Christian:* If I were one of thy children, thou wouldst not hide thyself from me as thou dost.

*Jesus:* I have hid myself and my face from some of my prophets and people of old, and yet it was in love to them, and so it is to thee (Ps. 88:14; Isa. 8:17; 94:7).

*Christian:* But thou hast hid thyself from me, and thou seemest also to be angry with me (Isa. 54:7; Jer. 31:9).

*Jesus:* Fury is not with me (towards thee) and, though I be angry, yet my anger is but for a moment (Isa. 27:4; 54:8).

*Christian:* Yet, Lord, thou hast been angry with me a long time, for thou hast forgotten me.

*Jesus:* Zion did say so, "the Lord hath forsaken me, and my Lord hath forgotten me" (Jer. 51:5); yet I had not forgot her; for she was graven upon the balms of my hands (Isa. 49:15-16).

*Christian:* But, Lord, if thou hast not forgotten me, thou wouldst never have left me in such a wilderness and barren condition as I am in.

Looking unto Jesus

*Jesus:* I have allured thee into the wilderness, that I might speak comfortably unto thee (Hos. 2:14).

*Christian:* I have been many years in trouble and terrors, and wanting peace in my soul, which could not possibly have been, if I had truly believed in thee.

*Jesus:* But now I will speak peace unto thee, and I will guide thee into the way of peace (Ps. 85:8; Luke 1:79).

*Christian:* Lord, wilt thou speak peace unto me, and guide me in the way of peace?

*Jesus:* I will create the fruit of thy lips, "peace, peace," and my Spirit shall be in thee, and his fruit shall be peace unto thy soul (Isa. 55:12; 56:19).[11]

*Christian:* But, Lord, thy word [says] there is no peace to the wicked.

*Jesus:* No, not to a man that will persist in his wicked way, and doth not, nor will not believe in me; but thou art one of those that I bore chastisement of thy peace, and one of the children of peace (Isa. 53:5; 54:13).

*Christian:* But, Lord, how can I have peace, seeing a man cannot have peace before (and without) he doth believe?

*Jesus:* Thou shalt have faith and peace, and I will give peace through believing (2 Thess. 3:6, 16).

*Christian:* But, Lord, then I must know that I am one of thine.

*Jesus:* Thou shalt know that I am the Lord, thy God, and that thou art one of my people (Ezek. 34:30).

*Christian:* O, how shall I know that?

*Jesus:* My Spirit shall bear witness with thy spirit that thou art my child (Rom. 8:16).

*Christian:* But how shall I know that it is thy Spirit that beareth this witness, and that it is not the spirit of delusion?

*Jesus:* Thou mayest know by its power in working in thy heart, which no other Spirit can work alike; as also by the earnest and fruits thereof (2 Cor. 5:5; 7:22;[12] Gal. 5:22–23).

---

11. Isa 56:19 does not exist.—ed.

12. 2 Cor 7:22 does not exist.—ed.

*Christian:* Lord, what else shall I believe, besides being one of thine?

*Jesus:* Dost thou believe that?

*Christian:* Yes, Lord, I do believe that thou art Jesus, the Son of God, and the Savior of the world (John 6:69; 11:27; Acts 8:37).

*Jesus:* But dost thou believe that I am thy Savior?

*Christian:* Lord, I do believe that there is no other way to be saved but only by thee (Acts 4:12).

*Jesus:* But dost thou believe that thou shalt be saved by me?

*Christian:* Lord, I do believe; help my unbelief (Mark 9:24).

*Jesus:* To thee it is given to believe (Phil. 1:29).

*Christian:* Now, Lord, I do believe.

*Jesus:* What dost thou now believe?

*Christian:* I believe that thou lovest me, and didst give thyself for me (Gal. 2:20), and that thou art my Lord and my God (John 20:28), and that I am justified and shall be saved by grace (Acts 15:11).

*Jesus:* How camest thou to believe this?

*Christian:* Lord, it is by thy gift and work that I do believe it (Eph. 2:8; Heb. 12:2).

*Jesus:* Well now [that] thou dost believe, what wilt thou do?

*Christian:* Lord, what wilt thou have me to do (Acts 9:6)?

*Jesus:* If thou lovest me, keep my words (John 14:23).

*Christian:* What are those words of thine?

*Jesus:* Search the Scriptures, for they are able to make thee perfect and wise unto salvation, and to furnish thee for every good work (John 5:39; 2 Tim. 3:16–17).

*Christian:* But Lord, how shall I understand thy word?

*Jesus:* I will make known my word unto thee (Prov. 1:23).

*Christian:* But Lord, is there no danger of my departing and falling away from thee now I do believe?

*Jesus:* No. The mountains shall depart, and the hills be removed, but my lovingkindness shall not depart from thee (Isa. 54:10; Jer. 32:41).

## Looking unto Jesus

*Christian:* Lord, I will keep thy precepts with my whole heart (Phil. 1:19, 29).

*Jesus:* I have redeemed thee that thou shouldest serve me without fear, in holiness and righteousness, all the days of thy life (Luke 1:6).

*Christian:* Come ye children and I will declare what the Lord hath done for my soul (Ps. 34:11). My soul shall make her boasts [in] the Lord; the humble shall hear this and be glad; O magnify the Lord with me, and let us exalt his name together (Ps. 34:2–3).

# 4

# The Christ-Centered Piety of Vavasor Powell[1]

According to John Newton, the goal of preaching is "to break a hard heart and to heal a broken heart."[2] That is to say, the goal of preaching is to convict the comfortable sinner and comfort the convicted sinner. In seeking to fulfill this calling, the preacher must understand that he faces a diverse audience. First, there is the *troubled penitent*. He is an unbeliever, who feels the weight of his sin. He is gripped by the fact that he has offended a holy God. Secondly, there is the *moral hypocrite*. He is an unbeliever, who thinks all is well with his soul. He is self-righteous, because he has never seen himself in the light of God's law. Thirdly, there is the *anxious disciple*. He is a believer, who sees more of his sin than God's grace. He sees more of his unfaithfulness than God's faithfulness. He sees more of his unworthiness than Christ's worthiness.

As the preacher stands before his congregation, these three individuals are present. They have different ailments, requiring different remedies. This poses one of the most challenging (and potentially discouraging) aspects of

---

1. Much of this chapter's content was originally presented as a paper at the annual conference of the Andrew Fuller Center (Southern Baptist Theological Seminary, Louisville, KY), August 2009.

2. As quoted in Stott, *Between Two Worlds*, 314.

pastoral ministry.³ How does the preacher meet this challenge? For insight, we turn to a little-known Welsh pastor, Vavasor Powell.⁴

> He was born of one of the best families in Wales, 1617; was graduated at Christ College, Oxford, and entered the Established Church, as curate to his uncle, in Shropshire.⁵ One day a Puritan reproved him for breaking the Sabbath by taking part in the "Sports," and this led to his conversion after two years of mental agony for his sins.⁶ In 1641 he began to preach the Gospel in earnest, but, his life being threatened, he fled to London in 1642, and joined the Parliamentary army as chaplain. After preaching two years in Kent he returned to Wales, bearing a certificate from the Assembly of Divines as an accredited preacher⁷ . . . He was constantly in the pulpit and the saddle, preaching two or three times a day, in two or three places,⁸ during the fourteen years of his liberty, 1646–1660 . . . Powell was immersed and became a Baptist in 1656.⁹ In his "Confession of Faith" he teaches that baptism is immersion, and believers its only subjects; but he did not hold it as the boundary of Church communion, nor were his Churches in the Baptist Association. Notwithstanding this, no man fired the hatred of the Church party as he did, and no man's character was more aspersed

---

3. Compounding this challenge is the problem of misinterpretation. The preacher speaks to people, who are prone to apply to themselves what is intended for others. As Richard Baxter expresses it, "It is a very hard thing for us to write or preach to one party, but the other will misapply it to themselves, and make an ill use of it" (*Christian Directory*, 1:277). In the context, Baxter is speaking of "over-scrupulous" people, who misapply his teaching on Christian moderation. However, the principle holds true for the present discussion. Misinterpretation accounts in part for some of the charges that are often levied against the Puritans. Some have misinterpreted the Puritans' exhortation to the *troubled penitent* and accused them of *antinomianism*. Others have misinterpreted the Puritans' exhortation to the *moral hypocrite* and accused them of *legalism* and *preparationism*. Others have misinterpreted the Puritans' exhortation to the *anxious disciple* and accused them of *introspectionism*.

4. This description is found in Armitage, *History of the Baptists*, 600–601. As for Powell's theological persuasion, see his *The Scripture's Concord*. This tract consists of a series of 256 questions and answers, in which his Reformed convictions are evident.

5. Shropshire is a county in the West Midlands.

6. According to Edward Bagshawe, Powell was converted through hearing Walter Cradock's sermons and through reading Richard Sibbe's *The Bruised Reed* (*Life and Death of Mr. Vavasor Powell*, 1–14).

7. This certificate included the names of fifteen Westminster divines.

8. By later admirers, Powell has been called "the Whitefield of Wales."

9. For more on Powell's "Baptist" associations, see Coulton, "Vavasor Powell and his Baptist Connections," 477–87.

than his, till death relieved him, October 27th, 1671 . . . Many of his troubles sprang from his resistance of Cromwell's later assumptions.[10] He had denounced him from the pulpit in Blackfriars,[11] for which cause he was arrested.[12] He suffered every kind of persecution for preaching, and spent eight years in thirteen prisons, dying in the Fleet.[13]

During his years of ministry, Vavasor Powell wrote a number of small tracts and treatises.[14] The focus of this chapter is his *Saving Faith Discovered in Three Heavenly Conferences*, in which he records three fictional conversations.[15] The first is between Christ and the Publican (the *troubled penitent*); the second is between Christ and the Pharisee (the *moral hypocrite*); and the third is between Christ and the Doubting Christian (the *anxious disciple*).[16] Through these discussions, Powell makes it clear that the preacher only reaches his diverse audience by persistently pointing to Christ in his manifold roles and relations.

---

10. Powell openly opposed Oliver Cromwell's decision to become Lord Protector.

11. A district in central London, named after black-garmented Dominican Friars, who resided in the area as early as the thirteenth century.

12. For the theory that it was Powell's "millenarian" views more than anything else that led to his trouble, see Milton, "The Pastoral Predicament of Vavasor Powell." Powell was a Fifth Monarchist. According to this movement, the statue in Nebuchadnezzar's dream (Dan 2) symbolizes the rise and fall of four kingdoms. The stone that crushes the statue is a fifth kingdom, belonging to Christ. The Fifth Monarchists interpreted this kingdom in terms of an earthly millennial reign, and eventually viewed Cromwell's "protectorship" as an impediment to its establishment.

13. I.e., the Fleet Prison, London. Powell was buried in Bunhill Fields, London.

14. These include: *The Scriptures Concord* (1646); *The Threefold State of an Elect Person* (1646); *God the Father Glorified* (1649); *Christ's and Moses' Excellency, or Zion's and Sinai's Glory* (1650); *Saving Faith Discovered in Three Heavenly Conferences* (1651); *Christ Exalted above All Creatures by God His Father* (1651); *Common-Prayer-Book No Divine Service* (1660); *The Bird in the Cage* (1661); *The Sufferers Catechism* (1664); and *A New and Useful Concordance to the Holy Bible* (1671).

15. Although much of the content is biblical, the conversations themselves are fictional.

16. The subject of the "Publican and Pharisee" is popular among the Puritans. By way of example, see Bunyan, *Discourse upon the Pharisee and the Publican*. This treatise is an exposition of Luke 18:10–13. Bunyan describes the Publican and Pharisee as "two men in whose condition the whole world is comprehended" (*Works*, 10:111). He describes Christ's goal in this discourse as "the conviction of the proud and self-conceited Pharisee" and "the raising up and healing of the cast-down and dejected Publican" (*Works*, 10:114).

## THE PUBLICAN (TROUBLED PENITENT)

In the first conversation, Powell begins with Christ's invitation: "If any man thirst, let him come unto me, and drink."[17] What is the context for this invitation? It is the last day of the Feast of Booths (or Tabernacles).[18] The worshippers leave their booths at daybreak. Once at the temple, they divide into three groups. The first remains at the temple, where they prepare the sacrifice. The second heads to Moza, where they cut down willow branches for adorning the altar. The third heads to the pool of Siloam, where a priest fills a golden pitcher with water. Having returned to the temple, this priest is joined by another priest, who has the wine for the drink offering. Together, they ascend the altar. At the east side, there is a funnel for the wine. At the west side, there is a funnel for the water. They pour the water and wine into the funnels. Immediately following, the people sing the Hallel.[19]

The temple stands in all its grandeur. The willow branches adorn the altar. The smoke from the burnt offering ascends in a cloud. The last drops of water and wine cascade down the altar. The final words of the Hallel ascend from the people: "Save now, I beseech thee, O LORD." In this context, Christ extends his invitation: "If any man thirst, let him come unto me and drink." In so doing, he makes it clear that he alone can satisfy humanity's spiritual thirst. In order to grasp how, we must understand the Feast of Booths. The pouring of the water points to a particular incident in Israel's history. At Meribah, the Israelites sin by grumbling against God on account of the lack of water. God says to Moses, "Behold, I will stand before thee there upon the rock in Horeb; and thou shalt smite the rock, and there shall come water out of it, that the people will drink."[20] God stands on the rock, thereby identifying with it. Moses strikes the rock with his rod. Symbolically, therefore, God bears the judgment for the people's sin. Then, the water flows from the rock to satisfy their thirst.[21] When Christ cries, "Come to me," he identifies himself as the Rock—the one who is wounded for our transgressions and crushed for our iniquities.[22] As such, he reconciles us to God, thereby restoring that for which we thirst—fellowship with God.

17. John 7:37. Powell, *Saving Faith*, 39.

18. For the details in this section, see Edersheim, *Life and Times of Jesus the Messiah*, 4:156–61.

19. Pss 113–18.

20. Exod 17:6.

21. See Deut 32:4–31; Pss 78:35 and 95:1.

22. Isa 53:5. Flavel expresses the significance of this statement as follows: "Lord, the

## The Publican's Thirst

In the dialogue that follows, Powell makes it clear that the Publican responds to Christ's invitation because of his thirst. In other words, he is aware of his sin, and desires righteousness. His attitude is that which Christ describes in the Beatitudes.[23] To begin with, the Publican is "poor in spirit."[24] That is to say, he recognizes that he is without moral virtues adequate to commend himself to God. This poverty of spirit causes him to mourn. He is troubled by the very nature of sin. He perceives sin's opposition to God, and grieves because of it. In turn, his sorrow leads to meekness—humility in God's presence. His proper self-assessment obliterates his self-assurance and self-reliance. In this condition, he hungers and thirsts after righteousness. For Powell, such "hungering and thirsting" is an essential ingredient of saving faith.

Powell shares this conviction with his fellow Puritans. In *The Pilgrim's Progress*, John Bunyan provides a powerful illustration of the importance of hungering and thirsting after righteousness. Pilgrim and Pliable set out for the Celestial City. Soon after, they veer from the path, and fall into the Slough of Despond. Pliable is so dejected and disappointed that he decides to return home. Why? The answer is found in what he says to Pilgrim, while they are struggling in the Slough: "Is this the happiness you have told me all this while of?"[25] The question is revealing. It shows that Pilgrim and Pliable embark on the journey for very different reasons. (1) Pliable's reason is

---

condemnation was thine, that the justification might be mine; the agony thine, that the victory might be mine; the pain was thine, and the ease mine; the stripes thine, and healing balm issuing from them mine; the vinegar and gall were thine, that the honey and sweet might be mine; the curse was thine, that the blessing might be mine; the crown of thorns was thine, that the crown of glory might be mine; the death was thine, the life purchased by it mine; thou paidst the price that I might enjoy the inheritance" (*Works*, 1:101).

23. Matt 5:3–6.

24. William Perkins describes poverty of spirit as follows: "Finding no goodness in their hearts, they despair in themselves, and fly wholly to the mercy of God in Christ, for grace and comfort" (*Christ's Sermon in the Mount*, 3:4). Later Puritans are in full agreement. George Swinnock describes the poor in spirit as the "broken-hearted," who possess a "hungry soul" (*Works*, 1:206). Robert Harris says that poverty of spirit describes the individual who looks "into his spiritual state, and there finds himself worse than nothing, and thereupon makes to God for a spiritual supply, and is willing to take it upon any term" (*Way of True Happiness*, 28). Similarly, in defining the poor in spirit, Thomas Watson refers to "those who are brought to the sense of their sins, and seeing no goodness in themselves, despair in themselves and sue wholly to the mercy of God in Christ" (*Beatitudes*, 42).

25. Bunyan, *Pilgrim's Progress*, 8.

*carnal*. He does not have any sense of his sin. He does not have any burden on his back. In a word, he is motivated by self-interest.[26] When the way becomes difficult, and his perceived *interests* are not met, he becomes disillusioned. Unsurprisingly, he turns back. (2) Pilgrim's reason is *spiritual*. He is conscious of his sin—the burden on his back. He is looking for someone, who is able to save him from his sin. He is hungering and thirsting after righteousness. Therefore, nothing will deter him from his pursuit.

Bunyan's (and Powell's) point is that we must perceive our real need, in order to come to Christ. We must be "thirsty" before we will drink of Christ. We must be "hungry" before we will feed on Christ. We must be "weary and heavy-laden" before we will rest in Christ.[27] We must be like a "battered reed" (i.e., easy to break off) and a "smoldering wick" (i.e., easy to put out) before we will turn to Christ.[28] For Powell, there must be humiliation for sin before there will ever be faith in Christ. That is the Publican's condition. He feels his sin. He knows his need. Having heard that Christ is "a friend of publicans and sinners,"[29] he comes to him.

## Christ the Shepherd

Powell continues to describe the conversation between Christ and the Publican. Christ asks him what he knows of his teaching. The Publican recounts

---

26. There is an example of this "self-interest" in John 6. Christ performs a sign (or miracle) by feeding the multitude with five loaves and two fish. The people respond by identifying Christ as "the prophet that should come into the world" (verse 14). See Deut 18:15. In their minds, Christ is the second Moses. They think he will deliver them from the Romans, as Moses delivered their ancestors from the Egyptians. They are looking for a political figure to meet their *felt* needs. But they fail to appreciate the sign's true character. For this reason, Christ withdraws from them. But they are persistent. They follow him to the other side of the sea, where Christ says to them: "Verily, verily, I say unto you, Ye seek me, not because ye saw the miracles, but because ye did eat of the loaves, and were filled" (verse 26). In other words, they follow him out of self-interest. He challenges them to strive for spiritual, not physical, food. It is through faith, assimilating him spiritually, as physical bread is assimilated physically, that they will receive eternal life (verses 27–29). But they are not interested. As F. F. Bruce declares, "What they wanted, he would not give; what he offered, they would not receive" (*Gospel and Epistles of John*, 164). As long as they think Christ is ready to cater to their wants, they are enthusiastic. But the moment they perceive his real message and his real purpose, they abandon him. The natural man always flocks to a man-centered Christ and a man-centered gospel.

27. Matt 11:28–30.
28. Matt 12:20.
29. Powell, *Saving Faith*, 40.

the parables of the lost sheep, lost coin, and lost son,[30] but acknowledges that he does not understand their significance. Christ explains that these "comparisons" are intended to "comfort and encourage the publicans and great sinners."[31] He immediately presents himself to the Publican in a manner that is commensurate with his need, pointing to himself as "the Savior of sinners, and the Shepherd of the sheep."[32] The context, of course, is John 10, where the Jewish religious leaders are perplexed by Christ's healing of the blind man. They cannot explain it. When the man declares that he believes Christ is from God, they cast him out—excommunicate him.[33] In marked contrast to these false shepherds, Christ claims, "I am the good shepherd."[34] As opposed to the "stranger," he knows his sheep.[35] As opposed to the "thief," he blesses his sheep.[36] As opposed to the "hireling," he dies for his sheep.[37] Christ is emphasizing the fact that he (unlike the Jewish religious leaders) acts out of love—in the best interest of his sheep.

Despite Christ's assurances, the Publican expresses numerous uncertainties. Christ responds to each in turn.[38] (1) The Publican is wicked, but Christ calls sinners. (2) The Publican is exceedingly wicked, but Christ forgives enormous debts. (3) The Publican is a rebel, but Christ delivers those who are in bondage to sin. (4) The Publican is the greatest sinner, but Christ is abundantly merciful. (5) The Publican has wearied God with his sin, but Christ forgives for his own name's sake. (6) The Publican's sins are unforgivable, but Christ forgets sins. (7) The Publican is the son of wicked parents, but Christ does not judge anyone for his parents' sins. (8) The Publican is an old sinner, but Christ calls sinners at the last hour. (9) The Publican has multiplied sins, but Christ multiplies pardons. (10) The Publican has enticed others to sin, but Christ transforms sinners into leaders in the way of righteousness. (11) The Publican has persecuted Christians, but Christ shows mercy to those who sin ignorantly through unbelief. (12) The Publican is a hardened and habitual sinner, but Christ softens the hardest heart.

30. Ibid., 40–41. See Luke 15:3–32.
31. Powell, *Saving Faith*, 41.
32. Ibid.
33. John 9:34.
34. John 10:11.
35. John 10:5.
36. John 10:10.
37. John 10:12.
38. Powell, *Saving Faith*, 41–44.

Through this exchange, the Publican begins to comprehend the nature of saving grace. He sees that he has never done anything to merit God's favor. He sees that he is completely dependent upon Christ. He cries, "Lord, wilt thou do all for me?"[39] Christ responds by showing him what he has done.[40] He was equal with God, yet he became a servant. He was the possessor of heaven and earth, yet he became poor. He was honored, yet he became forsaken. He was sinless, yet he became sin. He was the law-giver, yet he became a curse. He was the life-giver, yet he became a sacrifice. He was the Father's delight, yet he became the object of divine wrath. Christ tells the Publican that he did all of these things on his behalf. The Publican was an enemy of God, but Christ made peace. The Publican was a slave of the devil and a firebrand of hell, but Christ rescued him from the power of the one and redeemed him from the punishment of the other. He assures the Publican: "Thou didst not deserve it, but yet I did it freely and out of love to thee."[41] Christ follows this up with another charge: "If thou wilt believe, and trust wholly and only upon me, and upon my righteousness and merits, thou shalt be saved."[42] The Publican is still hesitant, because he does not want to be guilty of presumption. But Christ assures him that it is not presumption to do what he commands.[43] Finally, the Publican believes.[44]

## THE PHARISEE (MORAL HYPOCRITE)

Next, Powell describes Christ's dialogue with the Pharisee. He begins with the Pharisee's question: "What shall we do, that we might work the works of God?"[45] As in the case of the Publican, Christ tells the Pharisee that he must believe in him. But the language of faith is meaningless to someone who thinks his salvation depends upon his own effort. Therefore, the Pharisee simply rephrases his question: "But, Master, what good thing shall I do,

39. Ibid., 45.
40. Ibid., 45–46.
41. Ibid., 46.
42. Ibid., 46.
43. Ibid.
44. The conversation does not end here. Immediately, two fears beset the Publican. (1) He is afraid that he might lose his faith. Christ declares that he is the author and finisher of faith (John 1:12; 4:14; 7:38–39). (2) He is afraid that he might sin again. Christ declares that he is the propitiation for sin (1 John 2:1–2, 12) (Powell, *Saving Faith*, 46–48).
45. Powell, *Saving Faith*, 48.

*The Christ-Centered Piety of Vavasor Powell*

that I may have eternal life?"[46] Christ replies by commanding him to keep the Ten Commandments. The Pharisee's response: "I have kept them all from my youth."[47] This bold claim leads Christ to question the Pharisee's understanding of three vital subjects.

The first is *the law*. The Pharisee thinks he has kept the Ten Commandments. But Christ reminds him that "they, which followed after the law of righteousness, have not attained to the law of righteousness."[48] In other words, the Pharisee deceives himself. He has not kept the Ten Commandments. Christ explains that the law condemns, but never justifies.[49] But the Pharisee is obstinate, declaring, "I hope rather to be justified than to be judged by the law."[50]

The second subject is *righteousness*.[51] Christ explains the difference between the righteousness of the law and the righteousness of faith.[52] The first pertains to those who think they can please God by obeying the law. The second pertains to those who, realizing that their righteousness is unacceptable in God's sight, look to Christ. The Pharisee asks, "How can men be saved by believing in thee, for thou art but one?"[53] Christ explains the doctrine of justification by grace alone through faith alone.[54] But the Pharisee will have none of it. He claims to follow Abraham, who (in his opinion) was justified by works.

The third subject is *works*. Christ takes the Pharisee to Scripture to show that God justified Abraham by faith apart from works.[55] He explains that Abraham's good works flowed from his faith.[56] Essentially, Christ tells

46. Ibid.
47. Ibid.
48. See Rom 9:31.
49. Powell, *Saving Faith*, 49–50.
50. Ibid., 50.
51. For Bunyan's description of the Pharisee's misunderstanding of righteousness, see *Works*, 10:124–28.
52. Powell, *Saving Faith*, 50. See Rom 2:26; 3:21; and 4:13.
53. Powell, *Saving Faith*, 51.
54. See Rom 5:9 and 1 Cor 1:30.
55. Powell, *Saving Faith*, 51. See Rom 4:3–16 and Gal 3:14–20.
56. The relationship between faith and works is a controversial subject. "We must," says Dane Ortlund, "continue to grapple with this thorny issue—lest we promote either presumptuousness (neglecting the judgment/works motif) or equally dangerous moralism (neglecting the justification/faith motif)" ("Justified by Faith," 323). Ortlund provides a helpful overview of fourteen ways in which this "paradox" has been handled throughout the centuries.

the Pharisee that his understanding of justification is a far cry from Abraham's experience. In this section of the dialogue, Powell quotes Romans 4, where the apostle Paul makes it clear that God justified Abraham apart from works.[57] Paul asks, "What shall we say then that Abraham our father, as pertaining to the flesh, has found?"[58] Abraham did not find (i.e., gain or achieve) anything by "the flesh" (i.e., his own effort); on the contrary, "Abraham believed God, and it was counted unto him for righteousness."[59] Paul proceeds to explain what it means to believe by contrasting two men. The first is "him that worketh."[60] This man receives his wage. It is not a gift, but something he has earned. The second man is "him that worketh not."[61] He does not receive a wage. If he receives anything, it is a gift. Paul's point is simply this: believing is the opposite of working.

Having clarified the meaning of these three (law, righteousness, and works), Christ draws out the implications as follows: "It is not for their well-doing that men are accepted with my Father, but they are made acceptable in me, and their works are accepted for my sake."[62] But the Pharisee is unmoved. He asks, "But am I no nearer heaven, that perform good works, than this sinful and ungodly publican?"[63]

## The Pharisee's Pride

At this point in the conversation, Powell makes it clear that the Pharisee's unwillingness to believe in Christ flows from his pride. The Pharisee rests in the fact that he is a child of Abraham.[64] But Christ is blunt: "If ye were Abraham's children, ye would do the works of Abraham."[65] Abraham

57. Rom 4:1–8.
58. Rom 4:1.
59. Rom 4:3. Here, Paul quotes Gen 15:6, where God promises Abraham that he will have a son, and that his descendents will be as numerous as the stars.
60. Rom 4:4.
61. Rom 4:5.
62. Powell, *Saving Faith*, 52. See Eph 1:6 and 1 Pet 2:6.
63. Powell, *Saving Faith*, 52.
64. See John 7:49 and 8:33.
65. John 8:39. Their obstinacy is prevalent throughout John 8. (1) In verses 21–25, Christ tells them that they are from below and of this world. They respond *intellectually*: "Who art thou?" (2) In verses 26–33, he tells them that they are enslaved to sin. They respond *emotionally*: "We be Abraham's seed." (3) In verses 34–48, he tells them that they are children of Satan. They respond *personally*: "Thou art a Samaritan, and hast a demon."

believed. The Pharisee fails to do just that. Therefore, Christ warns him of his folly. (1) He informs the Pharisee that he is in bondage to sin.[66] Christ alone can set him free. By his death, he satisfies the law. By his resurrection, he overcomes death. By his Spirit, he subdues sin. But the Pharisee still refuses to listen: "Sir, I hope to be freed another way, to wit, by my sacrifices, prayers, and good works."[67] (2) Christ informs the Pharisee that his works are repugnant in God's sight.[68] Simply put, they are an "abomination." Why? Their root is corrupt.[69] But the Pharisee turns a deaf ear: "I do not fear what thou sayest, for I am better persuaded of myself."[70] (3) Christ informs the Pharisee that his motives are hypocritical.[71] God rejects his praying, fasting, and giving, because he seeks "the honor of men, and not the honor which cometh from God."[72]

---

(4) In verses 49–59, he tells them that they are in darkness. They respond *physically*: "Then took they up stones to cast at him."

66. Powell, *Saving Faith*, 52. See John 8:34–36, 44.
67. Powell, *Saving Faith*, 52.
68. Ibid., 52–53.
69. This view of the effect of Adam's fall is known as the Augustinian principle, which Calvin articulates as follows: "The natural gifts in men were corrupted, but the supernatural taken away" (*Institutes*, 2.2.4, 12, 14, 18). The "natural gifts" are the faculties of the soul, whereas the "supernatural gifts" are knowledge, righteousness, and holiness (Eph 4:24; Col 3:10). Calvin never denies the fallen will's ability to choose between good and evil (*Institutes*, 1.5.6; 2.1.11; 2.2.13; 2.3.3; 3.14.2); rather, he denies that the fallen will's choice of good is good in God's sight. By virtue of the fall, humanity has lost the image of God. Therefore, when people use their faculties in choosing between good and evil, they fail to do so from a right principle. For this reason, their choices are never good in God's sight. Whether a deed is good or evil is determined by the desire from which it flows. Unbelievers do not love God; therefore, their deeds are never good in God's sight.
70. Powell, *Saving Faith*, 53.
71. Ibid., 53. When it comes to the religious life, we must be careful to avoid hypocrisy (a desire to please people) and pursue sincerity (a desire to please God). Swinnock warns, "There is much counterfeit coin in the world, that goeth current among men, as if it were as good as the best; so there is a great deal of counterfeit holiness in the world, a great deal of civility, of morality, of common grace, which is taken for (or rather mistaken) by men for true saving grace; much fancy is taken for faith, presumption for hope, self-love for saint-love, and worldly sighs for godly sorrow" (*Works*, 3:287).
72. Powell, *Saving Faith*, 54. In the Sermon on the Mount, Christ demonstrates that the Pharisee is rigorous in his observance of the law, plus conscientious in his giving, praying, and fasting (Matt 6:1–18). In Swinnock's view, the Pharisee is "famous for gifts and parts," but "infamous for profaneness." On that basis, he cautions that it is possible to "pray like a saint, to preach like an angel, and yet to practice like a devil" (*Works*, 5:53–54).

This final warning appears to have a sobering effect upon the Pharisee. He declares, "Thy words begin to terrify me."[73] Again, Christ exhorts him to believe. The Pharisee wants to know how.[74] Christ gives a threefold response. (1) The Pharisee must see himself as the greatest and vilest of sinners. (2) The Pharisee must see his own righteousness as filthy "menstrual rags." (3) The Pharisee must cry, "Master, save me, or else I perish." In all this, Christ makes it clear that only the sick seek a physician. This is the Pharisee's real problem: he refuses to admit that he is spiritually sick.

Powell depicts Christ as driving his point home: "For I say unto you, that except your righteousness shall exceed the righteousness of the scribes and Pharisees, ye shall in no case enter into the kingdom of heaven."[75] In the context, Christ uses six antitheses to demonstrate that the scribes and Pharisees distort the meaning of the law by restricting it to *deeds*.[76] The Pharisee's misinterpretation of the law never leads him to a proper understanding of sin and righteousness. Consequently, it never stirs in him a real sense of his need. But Christ expounds the true significance of the law, making it clear that it is not merely concerned with *deeds* but *desires*. In this way, he seeks to impress upon the Pharisee the full extent of his sin. Elsewhere, he compares the Pharisee to a cup that is clean on the outside yet full of dirt, and a tomb that is beautiful on the outside yet full of bones.[77] In short, the Pharisee is more concerned about his appearance before men than before God. To put it another way, he places more emphasis on *externals* than *internals*.[78] As long as the Pharisee insists on clinging to his self-righteousness, he will never perceive his need for a Savior.[79] Therefore, he will never believe in Christ.

---

73. Powell, *Saving Faith*, 54.

74. Ibid., 54.

75. Matt 5:20.

76. Matt 5:21–48. Martyn Lloyd-Jones describes the antitheses as "six illustrations of one truth," namely, "Conformity to the law must not be thought of in terms of actions only. Thoughts, motives and desires are equally important" (*Sermon on the Mount*, 1:217).

77. Matt 23:5–8.

78. Perkins comments, "The inward righteousness of the heart they nothing regarded, thinking that perfect righteousness consisted in outward obedience, and by that they looked to be saved" (*Christ's Sermon in the Mount*, 3:41). Likewise, Swinnock remarks, "Their actions, to the eye of man, good, but their affections were bad; their practices did not proceed from renewed and gracious principles. Whatsoever civility was without in the life, there was no real sanctity within in the heart" (*Works*, 4:133).

79. The peril of self-righteousness is evident in Christ's story of the prodigal son in Luke

*The Christ-Centered Piety of Vavasor Powell*

Christ presses his argument even further, declaring that many will be surprised when they stand before him on the judgment day, because they have built on a "false foundation."[80] He means they trust in their own works.[81] But this foundation will not withstand God's judgment.[82] Upon hearing this, the Pharisee appears despondent: "I see thou dost reject me. I thought to be one of thy disciples, and to follow thee." Christ assures him that he does not reject him. On the contrary, it is the Pharisee who rejects Christ. But he remains unmoved. "And he went away sorrowful, and followed him no more."[83]

## Christ the Judge

In this conversation, Powell depicts Christ as the Judge, who warns the Pharisee: "I am he that searcheth the reins and hearts; and I will give unto

---

15:1–32. Tim Keller provides an insightful exposition in *The Prodigal God*. He maintains that the two brothers are the same, in that both rebel. The younger brother does so by doing *bad* things. The older brother does so by doing *good* things. Their actions are different; however, their motives are the same—selfishness. The older brother does not fall into flagrant sin, but he basks in his own self-righteousness. He does *good* things for the wrong reason. He is not motivated by love for his father, but self-centeredness. From the older brother's example, Keller warns, "We must repent of the things we have done wrong, but if that is all you do, you may remain just an elder brother. To truly become Christians we must also repent of the reasons we ever did anything right" (*Prodigal God*, 77–78).

80. Powell, *Saving Faith*, 55.

81. Christ proclaims, "I never knew you: depart from me, ye that work iniquity" (Matt 7:23). This charge raises a troubling question: How can Christ refer to people who preach in his name, cast out demons in his name, and perform miracles in his name, as *workers of iniquity*? A failure to love God mars all that we do—even good things. To help us better understand this, we need to distinguish between *civil* and *moral* goodness. An action may be *civilly* good (in man's sight) without being *morally* good (in God's sight). Whether an action is *morally* good or evil is determined by the principle from which it flows. If it does not flow from love for God, it is not *morally* good. It is for this reason that Christ refers to these people (who, from all appearances, do good things) as *workers of iniquity*. Christ's point in all this is to warn us not to rest in an *outward* appearance of godliness—no matter how good it looks. Instead, we must do his Father's will, meaning our lives must be marked by *new obedience* that flows from renewed affections.

82. Bunyan explains why self-righteousness is so damnable: "Wherefore this sin of trusting to his own righteousness is a most high and damning transgression; because it condemneth the righteousness of Christ, which is the only righteousness that is sufficient to save from the curse of the Law" (*Works*, 1:140).

83. Powell, *Saving Faith*, 56.

every one of you according to your works."[84] That is a very different approach from the one he takes with the Publican.[85] The Publican is thirsty; he is under conviction for sin. Therefore, Christ points to himself as the Shepherd of the sheep. The Pharisee, on the other hand, is not thirsty. He is not under conviction for sin. He does not perceive his need.[86] Christ cannot prescribe a remedy for an ailment the Pharisee does not acknowledge. More than anything else, the Pharisee must be convinced of his need. For this reason, Christ assumes the role of law-giver. He challenges the Pharisee: "Dost thou know the law?"

In Scripture, Christ takes a similar approach with the rich young ruler, who comes to him, asking, "What shall I do that I may inherit eternal life?"[87] Christ responds by quoting six commandments from the law. The young man claims, "Master, all these have I observed from my youth."[88] Christ replies, "One thing thou lackest: go thy way, sell whatsoever thou hast, and give to the poor, and thou shalt have treasure in heaven."[89] Christ is not suggesting that the young man can *do* something, in order to inherit eternal life; rather, he is correcting the young man's misunderstanding of the law. The young man thinks he is able to be justified by the law. Christ challenges his misunderstanding of the law's function, declaring, "Go thy way, sell whatsoever thou hast, and give to the poor." In this way, he reminds the young man of the foremost commandment: "Thou shalt have no other gods before me."[90] Christ is showing him that he has not kept the law,

---

84. Rev 2:23.

85. Regarding the Publican and Pharisee, Bunyan remarks, "They were, as you see, far from another in their own apprehension of themselves: one good, the other bad; but yet in the judgment of the Law, both alike, both the same, both sinners; for they both stood in need of merit" (*Works*, 10:114).

86. This was a serious issue in Powell's day, given the prevalence of what the Puritans call "civility." Swinnock explains, "If the unconverted person be one that lived civilly and orderly in his outward conversation—paying every man his own, keeping his church, forbearing enormous crimes, etc.—it will be then needful to commend his civility; Christ looked on such a man and loved him; but also to discover its defects and insufficiency, that there is one thing lacking; how his nature is universally polluted, and it must be thoroughly purified, or he is a lost man; that it is one thing to have a wound hid, and another thing to have it healed . . . They think all is well, their minds being darkened, and unable to discern and discover the secret lusts which are hugged in their hearts" (*Works*, 3:18).

87. Mark 10:17.

88. Mark 10:20.

89. Mark 10:21.

90. Exod 20:3.

and that he cannot keep the law. He is an idolater, in that he loves his money more than God. For Powell, that is the function of the law. It does not exist to tell us what we can do, but what we cannot do.

Powell stresses this approach because of his conviction that the knowledge of sin only comes through the law.[91] This is consistent with what the apostle Paul explains in Romans 7.[92] First, Paul affirms that the law reveals sin: "I had not known sin, but by the law."[93] He is not saying that he would have been ignorant of sin without the law,[94] but that he would have been ignorant of the *real* nature of sin without the law. By way of example, he appeals to the tenth commandment: "For I had not known lust, except the law had said, 'Thou shalt not covet.'"[95] Through this commandment, Paul realized that his desires are as damnable as his deeds.

Second, Paul affirms that the law provokes sin: "But sin, taking occasion by the commandment, wrought in me all manner of concupiscence. For without the law sin was dead."[96] When Paul says, "without the law sin was dead," he is speaking by way of comparison. Apart from the law, we sin. With the law, we sin even more. Why? It arouses obstinacy and hostility.[97]

---

91. This is why the Puritans place so much importance on preaching the law in a "searching" manner. In his exposition of Christ' words, "Ye are the salt of the earth" (Matt 5:13), Perkins explains that the application of God's Word to the soul must bear the "properties" of salt. (1) It must bite: "The Law must be applied to rip up men's hearts, to make them see their sins; it must fret and bite them by the curse thereof to cause them to renounce themselves." (2) It must season: "The Gospel must be preached, that men feeling their corruption, like rottenness in their souls; may by the blessing of the Spirit be thereby seasoned with grace, and so reconciled unto God, and made savoury in his sight." (3) It must preserve: "Both the Law and the Gospel must be continually dispensed, that thereby sin and corruption may be daily mortified and consumed both in heart and life; even as superfluous humours are dried up by salt" (*Christ's Sermon in the Mount*, 3:23).

92. Flavel provides an excellent summary of Rom 7:1–12: "The scope of the apostle in this epistle, and more particularly in this chapter, is to state the due use and excellence of the law, which he doth accordingly. First, By denying to it a power to justify us, which is the peculiar honor of Christ. Secondly, By ascribing to it a power to convince us, and so prepare us for Christ . . . It cannot make us righteous, but it can convince us that we are unrighteous; it cannot heal, but it can open and discover the wounds that sin hath given us" (*Works*, 2:287–88).

93. Rom 7:7.
94. See Rom 2:15.
95. Rom 7:7.
96. Rom 7:8.
97. See Rom.1:32 and 8:37.

Third, Paul affirms that the law condemns sinners: "For I was alive without the law once: but when the commandment came, sin revived, and I died."[98] There was a time when he was satisfied with his own self-righteousness, because he lacked a true knowledge of his sin through the law. However, the day arrived when the law came home with power, and sin became alive. The law revealed and provoked his sin. He died—he stood condemned in God's sight.

Powell is convinced, therefore, that the purpose of the law is to show us our sin.[99] Again, John Bunyan provides a helpful illustration of this truth. In *The Pilgrim's Progress*, he describes Christian is in the House of Interpreter, where he enters a large parlor, full of dust. A man enters and sweeps the dust. As a result, a cloud of dust fills the room. It is so thick that Christian begins to choke on it. Then, a woman enters. She sprinkles water on the dust and sweeps it away. Christian asks Interpreter what it all means. Interpreter explains that the parlor is the human heart, the dust is sin, the man is the law, and the woman is the gospel. The point is this: the law stirs sin, but it cannot subdue it.[100] The law shows us our filthiness, but it cannot cleanse us. The law shows us our wounds, but it cannot heal us. The law condemns us, but it cannot justify us.

Powell knows this is what the Pharisee needs to hear. The Pharisee trusts in his own righteousness, because he does not see himself in the light of God's law. For this reason, Powell stresses Christ's role as Judge. Christ takes the Pharisee to the law, in order to break his hard heart.[101] In the light of the law, the Pharisee must see his twofold need: (1) he needs someone to obey the law on his behalf; and (2) he needs someone to pay the penalty of the law on his behalf. In a word, he needs Christ.

---

98. Rom 7:9.

99. Generally speaking, the use of the law in preaching has fallen on hard times. Packer remarks, "Some will assure us that it is a waste of time preaching to modern hearers about the law and sin, for (it is said) such things mean nothing to them. Instead (it is suggested) we should just appeal to the needs which they feel already, and present Christ to them simply as One who gives peace, power and purpose to the neurotic and frustrated—a super-psychiatrist, in fact . . . Such preaching may soothe some, but it will help nobody; for a Christ who is not seen and sought as a Savior from sin will not be found to save from self or anything else" (*Quest for Godliness*, 164–65).

100. Bunyan, *Pilgrim's Progress*, 26–27.

101. This approach echoes Calvin: "The law is like a mirror. In it we contemplate our weakness, then the iniquity arising from this, and finally the curse coming from both—just as a mirror shows us the spots on our face. For when the capacity to follow righteousness fails him, man must be mired in sins" (*Institutes*, 2.7.7).

## THE DOUBTING CHRISTIAN (ANXIOUS DISCIPLE)

In the third conversation, Powell turns to Christ and the Doubting Christian.[102] He begins with Christ's invitation: "Come unto me, all ye that labor and are heavy laden, and I will give you rest."[103] Who are the "heavy laden"? They are those who feel the weight of their sin. Christ assures them that he welcomes them.

Christ's invitation provokes a cry from the Christian: "I feel I am unworthy to come unto thee; yea, unworthy of the least of thy mercies."[104] He proceeds to enunciate the causes of his uncertainty, but Christ addresses them all.[105] (1) He is a wretched sinner, but Christ is willing to account him worthy. (2) He finds nothing but evil in his heart, but Christ is a fountain where the filthy soul can be cleansed. (3) He sins against knowledge, but Christ forgives the most heinous sin.[106] (4) He sins without remorse, but Christ is able to see his "sense, shame, and sorrow." (5) He thinks he has committed the unpardonable sin, but Christ assures him that he has not. (6) He finds no power in his soul to resist sin, but Christ receives gifts from the rebellious. (7) He is hardened in sin, but Christ grants repentance. (8) He struggles with unbelief, but Christ knows these are Satan's "temptations and suggestions." (9) He faces a "thousand temptations," but Christ gives strength to overcome.[107] (10) His love is weak, but Christ circumcises the heart.[108] (11) He is fruitless, but Christ purges his people, so that they might bear fruit.[109]

## The Christian's Doubt

At this point in the conversation, Powell portrays a definite shift in the Christian's thinking; his concern moves from Christ's willingness to forgive sinners to Christ's willingness to forgive him. Given his condition, he feels as though

---

102. With this conversation, Powell enters unchartered waters, in that (unlike in the case of the Publican and the Pharisee) there is no *Doubting Christian* in the Bible. That being said, Powell attempts to draw on Scripture as the basis for this conversation.
103. Powell, *Saving Faith*, 56. See Matt 11:28.
104. Powell, *Saving Faith*, 56.
105. Ibid., 56–63.
106. Powell appeals to Peter and David as examples of this.
107. See 1 Cor 10:13; Heb 2:18; Jas 1:2; and 2 Pet 2:9.
108. See 1 John 4:19.
109. See John 15:4.

Christ has not forgiven him. He cries, "I have been many years in trouble and terrors, and wanting peace in my soul, which could not possibly have been, if I had truly believed in thee."[110] Simply put, he has professed faith for "many years," yet lacked "peace." He does not understand how his "wilderness" condition is consistent with faith in Christ. In short, he wants assurance.[111]

Christ replies by promising to guide the Christian into the way of peace (i.e., assurance). The Christian says he will only experience peace when he is convinced that he belongs to Christ.[112] Christ assures him: "My Spirit shall bear witness with thy spirit that thou art my child."[113] The Christian wants to know how he can discern the Spirit's witness. "Thou mayest know," says Christ, "by its power in working in thy heart, which no other Spirit can work alike; as also by the earnest and fruits thereof."[114]

In this exchange, Powell appeals to Romans 8, where the apostle Paul affirms that the sons of God have received "the Spirit of adoption."[115] The

---

110. Powell, *Saving Faith*, 64.

111. In the opinion of some, this crisis of assurance is self-induced among the Puritans. R. T. Kendall popularized this view by asserting that the *Westminster Confession of Faith* departs from Calvin's belief that "faith is *knowledge* ... merely witnessing what God has already done in Christ," and that assurance is "the *direct* act of faith" (*Calvin and English Calvinism*, 19–20, 25). Italics his. (For a similar position, see Hall, "Calvin Against the Calvinists," 19–37.) Kendall locates the primary cause of this departure in Theodore Beza's doctrine of limited atonement, for it "makes Christ's death that to which the decree of election has particular reference and that which makes the elect's salvation efficacious" (*Calvin and English Calvinism*, 29). He argues that William Perkins adopted Beza's distortions of Calvin's teaching, and his legacy ensured their inclusion at the Westminster Assembly where they received "creedal sanction" (*Calvin and English Calvinism*, 76). For critical reviews of Kendall's thesis, see Helm, "Calvin, English Calvinism and the Logic of Doctrinal Development," 179–85; Lane, Review of *Calvin and English Calvinism to 1649*, by R. T. Kendall, 29–31; and Reid, Review of *Calvin and English Calvinism to 1649*, by R. T. Kendall, 155–64. Joel Beeke adopts an entirely different view from Kendall in regards to the relationship between Calvin and the *Westminster Confession of Faith*, commenting, "The difference between Calvin and the Calvinists is substantial and developmental, but *not* antithetical as Hall and Kendall advocate" (*Assurance of Faith*, 20). Although the Puritans give practical and mystical syllogisms a more intrinsic role than Calvin, they continue to regard God's promises as the primary ground for assurance. Moreover, they distinguish between an initial act of faith and a fully developed assurance while insisting that the latter proceeds from the former. This "fully developed assurance" is what Powell describes in the case of the Doubting Christian.

112. Powell, *Saving Faith*, 64.

113. Ibid.

114. Ibid., 64. See 2 Cor 5:5 and Gal 5:22–23.

115. Rom 8:15.

"Spirit of slavery" produces terror as we see ourselves as God sees us, but the "Spirit of adoption" eases that terror by leading us to Christ.[116] The Holy Spirit then testifies with our spirit that we are sons of God—"heirs of God, and joint heirs with Christ."[117] How? For Powell, the answer is twofold.[118] First, the Holy Spirit testifies *subjectively*. That means he testifies internally as to our relationship with Christ.[119] Second, the Holy Spirit testifies *objectively*. He does so by producing fruit in us. The apostle John wrote his first epistle, "that [we] may know that [we] have eternal life."[120] How do we know? John points to three tests.[121] The first is theological—we must believe in God's Son. The second is relational—we must love God's people. The third is moral—we must keep God's commands.[122] The Holy Spirit works *objectively* in our lives by producing these three. In so doing, he testifies that we are indeed the sons of God.

Through the Holy Spirit's work, the Doubting Christian finally cries, "I believe that thou lovest me, and didst give thyself for me, and that thou art my Lord and my God, and that I am justified and shall be saved by grace."[123]

---

116. There are two schools of thought as to the "spirit of slavery." First, some believe it means *bondage to sin*. If so, Paul is saying we are no longer unregenerate, but regenerate. Second, some believe it means *conviction for sin*. According to this interpretation, both instances of the word *spirit* (in Rom 8:15) refer to the Holy Spirit. Therefore, the "spirit of slavery" is really the "Spirit of slavery." He brings us into bondage, when he convicts us of our sin. Having produced conviction and humiliation for sin, he then leads us to Christ, whereby we believe in him, and are adopted into God's family.

117. Rom 8:17.

118. Flavel asserts that the Holy Spirit testifies to our adoption in two ways. (1) "Objectively, i.e. by working those graces in our souls which are the conditions of the promise, and so the Spirit and his graces in us, are all one." (2) "The other way of the Spirit's witnessing is effectively, i.e. by irradiating the soul with a grace-discovering light, shining upon his own work" (*Works*, 5:434).

119. See Rom 5:5.

120. 1 John 5:13.

121. 1 John 3:23–24.

122. For the Puritans, there is no antithesis between law and gospel. We are not free from obeying the moral law, but free to obey it in accordance with the new covenant. This emphasis often results in the erroneous charge of *legalism*. However, as Ernest Kevan rightly acknowledges, "Legalism is the abuse of the Law as a means of obtaining a meritorious standing before God; it is the use of the Law 'as pharisaically conceived,' and an employment of it in its outward form without regard to its inward demands . . . The 'legalism' of Puritanism is a 'bogey' constructed by prejudiced imagination from the popular caricature of the God-fearing Puritan and from ignorance of what he taught" (*The Grace of Law*, 259).

123. Powell, *Saving Faith*, 35. See John 20:28; Acts 15:11; and Gal 2:20.

He asks Christ what he should do.[124] "If thou lovest me," says Christ, "keep my words."[125] The Christian pledges to keep Christ's precepts with his whole heart. With his new found assurance, he concludes with these words: "Come ye children and I will declare what the Lord hath done for my soul. My soul shall make her boasts in the Lord; the humble shall hear this and be glad; O magnify the Lord with me, and let us exalt his name together."[126]

## Christ the Husband

According to Powell, Christ takes an entirely different approach with the Doubting Christian than he does with the Publican and the Pharisee. Unlike the Pharisee, the Christian knows he is a sinner. Unlike the Publican, the Christian knows Christ forgives sinners. The problem for the Doubting Christian is whether or not Christ has forgiven *him*. Christ, therefore, comes to him from a different angle: "Fear not my spouse, for I am thy husband and thy father."[127] In other words, Christ declares ownership of the Christian,[128] claiming to act as his head.

When Adam and Eve disobeyed, they (along with all their posterity) fell into bondage to sin and death. By consequence, they fell under Satan's dominion. At that time, God ordained Satan to be the executioner of the sentence of death. Humanity's obligation to death is what gives Satan all his power. Obviously, the removal of that obligation is the termination of Satan's power. That is precisely what Christ accomplishes at the cross. He pays our debt by his death. In so doing, he destroys Satan's power.[129] The apostle Paul provides a concise description of this victory in Colossians 2. It involves three *stages*.

---

124. Powell, *Saving Faith*, 65.
125. See John 14:23.
126. Powell, *Saving Faith*, 66. See Pss 34:2–3, 11.
127. Powell, *Saving Faith*, 63.
128. This ownership is evident, for example, in Christ's high-priestly prayer in John 17. Repeatedly, Christ refers to those whom the Father has given him. What is so unique about these people? Christ gives them eternal life; he manifests God's name to them; he prays for them; and he shows them his glory (vv. 2, 6, 9, 24).
129. As Thomas Goodwin explains, "The power of Satan lies in sin, the power that sin hath over us lay in the law . . . Now, [Christ], by paying a price or sufficient ransom unto God for sin, the power of the law and devil all fell at once flat, and perished together" (*Works*, 5:304).

First, Christ removes our sin.[130] Paul declares, "And you, being dead in your sins and the uncircumcision of your flesh hath he quickened together with him, having forgiven you all trespasses."[131] This is the starting point for Christ's victory: he deals with our sin. Paul explains *how* in the preceding verse, affirming that we have been "buried with [Christ] in baptism."[132] Because we are one with Christ, his death is our death. That means we are no longer under sin's judicial penalty (or curse), because Christ has paid it in full. And, on that basis, God has "forgiven [us] all trespasses."

Second, Christ cancels our debt. Paul writes, "Blotting out the handwriting of ordinances that was against us, which was contrary to us, and he took it out of the way, nailing it to his cross."[133] As a result of our sin, we are condemned. However, Christ has taken that condemnation upon himself. Furthermore, Christ has fulfilled the righteousness of the law. Therefore, when we are united to him by faith, the penalty is removed and his righteousness is imputed to us. In this way, then, he has blotted out "the handwriting of ordinances that was against us, which was contrary to us."[134]

Third, Christ disarms our enemy. Paul declares, "And having spoiled principalities and powers, he made a show of them openly, triumphing over them in it."[135] At the cross, Christ broke Satan's power. He did so by taking away Satan's right to rule over us. Satan's rule is twofold: he rules *over* people by death,[136] and he rules *in* people by sin.[137] By his death, Christ destroyed Satan's rule. "All the power of Satan," writes John Owen, "consists in death, and those things that either conduce to it or do attend it. Now, death entered by sin, and therewithal the power of Satan. The Lord Jesus taking away sin and putting an end thereunto . . . the whole title of Satan falls and comes to nothing."[138] That is what Paul has in mind when he says that Christ "spoiled principalities and powers." By his death, he stripped them of their power. Having done so, he "made a show of them openly."[139]

---

130. For the term *remove* ("putting off"), see Col 2:11.
131. Col 2:13.
132. Col 2:12.
133. Col 2:14. See Eph 2:15.
134. Col 2:14.
135. Col 2:15. See Heb 2:14.
136. See Heb 2:14–15.
137. See Eph 2:2.
138. Owen, *Works*, 11:306–7.
139. By way of explanation, Thomas Goodwin states, "The allusion is manifestly unto

By his death at the cross, therefore, Christ has bruised the head of the serpent.[140] He has destroyed Satan's legal right to us. (1) Satan no longer has any claim upon us because Christ has paid our debt. (2) Satan no longer has any accusation against us because Christ has removed our guilt. Satan's power is death. Death's power is sin. But Christ has atoned for sin through his death thereby rendering Satan powerless. With that truth in view, Paul asks, "Who shall lay anything to the charge of God's elect? It is God that justifieth? Who is he that condemneth? It is Christ that died, yea rather, that is risen again, who is even at the right hand of God, who also maketh intercession for us?"[141] Here, Paul speaks of Christ's threefold work: his crucifixion, resurrection, and intercession. In light of this great work, Paul asks, "Who shall lay anything to the charge of God's elect?" Satan has no legal power (or right) to bring any charge against us. Christ lived for us, in that he fulfilled the law. Christ died for us, in that he paid the law's penalty for our sin. Christ intercedes for us, in that he guarantees our acceptance with the Father. Christ is seated at God's "right hand in the heavenly places, far above all principality, and power, and might, and dominion, and every name that is named, not only in this world, but also in that which is to come."[142] We share in his triumph by virtue of our union with him.

---

that Roman custom . . . after victories obtained, when the chief leader rode in triumph, leading the chieftains of the conquered enemy as an open spectacle" (*Works*, 5:305). Similarly, John Owen writes, "So he led captivity captive; or all the adverse powers of the salvation of the church, in triumph at his chariot wheels. I deny not but that his leading 'captivity captive' principally respects his spiritual conquest over Satan, and the destruction of his power; yet, whereas he is also said to 'spoil principalities and powers, making a show of them openly,' and triumphing over them, I no way doubt but Satan, the head of the apostasy, and the chief princes of darkness, were led openly, in sight of all the holy angels, as conquered captives,—the 'seed of the woman' having now bruised the 'head of the serpent'" (*Works*, 1:247-49).

140. Gen 3:15.
141. Rom 8:33-34.
142. Eph 1:21.

Christ is our husband, and we are his bride. Therefore, all that belongs to him becomes ours.[143] We are "heirs of God, joint heirs with Christ."[144] Equally true, all that belongs to us becomes his. (1) When we become one with Christ, our debt of sin becomes his. He pays it in full.[145] (2) When we become one with Christ, our wants become his. He meets our need for grace, righteousness, wisdom, peace, joy, and life.[146] (3) When we become one with Christ, our burdens become his. He bears them.[147] (4) When we become one with Christ, our afflictions become his. He governs them for our good.[148] (5) When we become one with Christ, our enemies become his. He has conquered sin, the devil, the world, and the grave.[149]

According to Powell, the Doubting Christian needs to hear that all he is (and has) is wrapped up in Christ. As a result of our union with Christ, we enjoy the benefits of the cross. Christ's forgiveness is greater than our sin. His merit is greater than our guilt. His strength is greater than our weakness. His humility is greater than our pride. His sufferings are greater than our failures. His fullness is greater than our want. His tenderness is greater than our temptation. His righteousness is greater than our vileness. Therefore, the Christian's assurance rests in Christ alone.

---

143. Flavel believes union with Christ is "a door opened to let in many rich blessings to the soul." That is to say, we participate in Christ's "spiritual privileges" (*Works*, 2:145–48). When Christ takes hold of us by his Spirit and we take hold of him by faith, we become one. By virtue of this mystical union, we partake of the blessings procured through the hypostatic union. We are one with Christ; therefore, we partake of the blessings of his prophetic office—he becomes to us wisdom. We are one with Christ; therefore, we partake of the blessings of his priestly office—he becomes to us righteousness. We are one with Christ; therefore, we partake of the blessings of his kingly office—he becomes to us sanctification and redemption. "These four," writes Flavel, "wisdom, righteousness, sanctification, and redemption, take in all that is necessary or desirable, to make a soul truly and perfectly blessed" (*Works*, 2:17). They make us "truly and perfectly blessed," because they correspond to "a fourfold misery lying upon sinful man, viz. ignorance, guilt, pollution, and the whole train of miserable consequences and effects, let in upon the nature of men, yea, the best and holiest of men, by sin" (*Works*, 2:16). For more on this, see Yuille, *The Inner Sanctum of Puritan Piety*, 45–53.

144. Rom 8:17.

145. Rom 6:23.

146. 2 Cor 12:9; 5:21; Col 2:3; John 14:27; 15:11; and 10:10.

147. 2 Cor 5:4 and Heb 4:15.

148. Rom 8:28.

149. Rom 8:3; Col 2:15; John 16:33; and 1 Cor 15:55–57.

## CONCLUSION

In these "three heavenly conferences," Powell's purpose is to demonstrate that Christ is sufficient for every need. (1) The Publican (the *troubled penitent*) needs Christ the Shepherd. He needs to hear that Christ is the righteousness of God for all who believe in him. He needs to hear that Christ came to save those who put no confidence in the flesh.[150] (2) The Pharisee (the *moral hypocrite*) needs Christ the Judge. He needs to hear the law's righteous demands. He needs to hear that he sins in word, thought, and deed. He needs to hear that his sin is heinous in God's sight. He needs to hear that he cannot do anything in his own strength to please a holy God. Until he sees this, he will never turn to Christ. (3) The Doubting Christian (the *anxious disciple*) needs Christ the Husband. He needs to hear that he stands to Christ in the same relation as the members of a physical body stand to their head, and Christ stands to believers in the same relation as the head of a physical body stands to its members.[151] As a result of this union, the body has communion with the head. In other words, Christians have communion with Christ. All those who are in Christ are righteous, because they are *one* with him—the righteousness of God.[152]

---

150. Phil 3:3.
151. See Eph 4:15–16.
152. See 1 Cor 1:30.

# Conclusion

CHRIST EXHORTS HIS DISCIPLES: "Abide in me, and I in you. As the branch cannot bear fruit of itself, except it abide in the vine; no more can ye, except ye abide in me."[1] A branch does not possess life in itself, but is completely dependent upon its relationship to the vine. Without that relationship, it dies. Similarly, Christ is the vine, and we are the branches. There is a vital, organic union between us. We must, therefore, abide in him, meaning we must cultivate close and constant communion with him. That is to say, we must continually look "unto Jesus the author and finisher of our faith."[2]

In the preceding chapters, I have attempted to explain what this *looking* implies. I have done so by turning to the Christ-centered piety of Thomas Wilcox and Vavasor Powell. To sum up, they teach us that we must behold Christ in his manifold roles and relations. As Redeemer, he delivers us from sin. As Mediator, he reconciles us to God. As Husband, he unites us to himself. As Father, he cares for us. As Priest, he intercedes for us. As Shepherd, he leads and protects us. As Prophet, he instructs and illuminates us. As Advocate, he pleads for us. As Friend, he loves us with fervent affection. As King, he rules over us. As Surety, he guarantees our inheritance. As

---

1. John 15:4. In this chapter, Christ begins with a metaphor. (1) There is the "true vine:" Christ (verse 1). He stands in marked contrast to Israel, which is identified in the OT as an unfruitful vine. (2) There is the "vinedresser:" God the Father (verse 1). What does he do? First, he "takes away" the branch that "does not bear fruit" (verse 2). Second, he "prunes" the branch that "bears fruit" (verse 2).

2. Heb 12:2. In what sense is Christ "the author and finisher of faith?" (1) Christ is the source of our faith. He purchases it for us, imparts it to us, and preserves it in us. (2) Christ is the example of our faith. The Greek word for "author" refers to someone who leads. See Heb 2:10. Christ leads by way of example, in that he lived a life of faith: in dependence upon God, in communion with God, in obedience to God, and in hope of things unseen. For confirmation, see John 6:57; 8:29; 15:10; and 16:28.

Rock, he satisfies us. "Look on [Christ]," urges Flavel, "in what respect or particular you will; cast your eye upon this lovely object, and view him any way; turn him in your serious thoughts which way you will; consider his person, his offices, his works, or any other thing belonging to him; you will find him altogether lovely."[3]

As Wilcox and Powell make clear, Christ's loveliness is magnified at the cross. Because of his love, he left a glorious crown, walked in our flesh, and took our infirmities. He gave sight to the blind, speech to the mute, hearing to the deaf, and life to the dead. He was hungry, thirsty, and weary. He was sorrowful unto death. He was betrayed, arrested, and condemned. He was crowned with thorns, scourged with whips, and pierced with nails. He hung on a shameful cross, bearing our guilt and shame. He submitted to desertion—that which we deserve for deserting God. He "poured out his soul unto death."[4] He was punished, so that we might be pardoned. He was cursed, so that we might be blessed. He was wounded, so that we might be healed. He was forsaken, so that we might be accepted. He was condemned, so that we might be justified.

For Wilcox and Powell, this makes Christ our *all in all*.[5] "He is," says Wilcox, "to bear the glory, for he alone is worthy. He is to build the temple of the Lord, and to bear the glory. He, by the Father's appointment, is the foundation-stone, corner-stone, and is to be the top-stone. He is the Father's fullness of grace and glory. Whatever your wants be, you may come to him. There is balsam enough in him fit for soul-cure."[6]

I trust that, in the forgoing pages, you have seen something of early Puritan (and Baptist) Christ-centered piety. And I pray (as Wilcox prayed centuries ago) that God has made this glimpse of Christ "like honey, sweet to your soul and health to your bones."[7]

---

3. Flavel, *Works*, 2:215. The expression "altogether lovely" is found in Song 5:16.
4. Isa 53:12.
5. 1 Cor 15:28.
6. Wilcox, *Guide to Eternal Glory*, 2.
7. Ibid.

# Bibliography

Alexander, Eric J. "The Supremacy of Jesus Christ." In *John Calvin: A Heart for Devotion, Doctrine, and Doxology*, edited by Burk Parsons, 109–18. Orlando: Reformation Trust, 2008.
Allison, C. F. *The Rise of Moralism: The Proclamation of the Gospel from Hooker to Baxter.* New York: Seabury, 1966.
Armitage, Thomas. *A History of the Baptists: Traced by Their Vital Principles and Practices, from the Time of Our Lord and Savior Christ to the Year 1886.* Paris, AR: Baptist Standard Bearer, 2001.
Bagshawe, Edward. *The Life and Death of Mr. Vavasor Powell, that Faithful Minister and Confessor of Christ.* London, 1671.
Baxter, Richard. *A Christian Directory.* Vol. 1, *The Practical Works of Richard Baxter.* 1846. Reprint, Morgan, PA: Soli Deo Gloria, 2000.
———. *The Practical Works of Richard Baxter: Select Treatises.* 1863. Reprint, grand Rapids: Baker, 1981.
Bayly, Lewis. *The Practice of Piety: Directing a Christian How to Walk, that He May Please God.* 1613. Reprint, Morgan, PA: Soli Deo Gloria, 2003.
Beeke, Joel. *Assurance of Faith: Calvin, English Puritanism, and the Dutch Second Reformation.* New York: Peter Lang, 1991.
———. "Personal Assurance of Faith: The Puritans and Chapter 18.2 of the Westminster Confession." *Westminster Theological Journal* 55 (1993) 1–30.
Bolton, Robert. *The Carnal Professor, Discovering the Woeful Slavery of a Man Guided by the Flesh.* 1634. Reprint, Ligonier, PA: Soli Deo Gloria, 1992.
———. *The Four Last Things: Death, Judgment, Hell, and Heaven.* 1633. Reprint, Morgan, PA: Soli Deo Gloria, 1994.
Bruce, F. F. *The Gospel and Epistles of John.* Grand Rapids: Eerdmans, 2001.
Bunyan, John. *A Discourse upon the Pharisee and the Publican.* Vol. 10, *The Miscellaneous Works of John Bunyan*, edited by Owen Watkins. Oxford: Clarendon, 1988.
———. *The Pilgrim's Progress.* Uhrichsville, OH: Barbour, 1985.
———. *A Treatise on the Fear of God.* 1679. Reprint, Morgan, PA: Soli Deo Gloria, 1999.
Burroughs, Jeremiah. *The Evil of Evils; or, The Exceeding Sinfulness of Sin.* London: Peter Cole, 1654.
Calvin, John. *Institutes of the Christian Religion.* Vol. 20–21, *The Library of Christian Classics*, edited by J. T. McNeill. Philadelphia: Westminster, 1960.

*Bibliography*

Charnock, Stephen. *Discourses Upon the Existence and Attributes of God*. 1853. Reprint, Grand Rapids: Baker, 1990.

Coulton, Barbara. "Vavasor Powell and his Baptist Connections." *Baptist Quarterly* 40/8 (2004) 477–87.

Crosby, Thomas. *The History of the English Baptists*. 4 vols. London, 1738–40.

Davies, Andrew. "The Holy Spirit in Puritan Experience." In *Faith and Ferment: Being Papers Read at the 1982 Conference*, 18–31. London: Westminster Conference, 1982.

Eaton, Michael. *No Condemnation: A New Theology of Assurance*. Downers Grove, IL: InterVarsity, 1995.

Edersheim, Alfred. *The Life and Times of Jesus the Messiah*. Iowa Falls, IA: World Publishers, 1990.

Flavel, John. *The Works of John Flavel*. 6 vols. 1820. Reprint, London: Banner of Truth, 1968.

Goodwin, Thomas. *The Works of Thomas Goodwin*. 1861. Reprint, Grand Rapids: Reformation Heritage, 2006.

Gouge, William. *Of Domesticall Duties: Eight Treatises*. London, 1622.

Gurnall, William. *The Christian in Complete Armour: A Treatise of the Saints' War against the Devil*. 1864. Reprint, Edinburgh: Banner of Truth, 1995.

Hall, Basil. "Calvin Against the Calvinists." In *John Calvin: A Collection of Distinguishing Essays*, edited by G. E. Duffield, 19–37. Grand Rapids: Eerdmans, 1966.

Hall, Joseph. *Christ Mystical; or, The Blessed Union of Christ and His Members*. London: Hodder and Stoughton, 1893.

Harris, Robert. *The Way of True Happiness, Delivered in Twenty-Four Sermons upon the Beatitudes*. Reprint, Morgan, PA: Soli Deo Gloria, 1998.

Haykin, Michael A. G. "Christ is All: Horatius Bonar (1808–1889) and his Christocentric Piety." *Eusebeia: The Bulletin of the Andrew Fuller Center* 3 (2004) 41–46.

Helm, Paul. "Calvin, English Calvinism and the Logic of Doctrinal Development." *Scottish Journal of Theology* 34 (1981) 179–85.

Helwys, Thomas. *The Life and Writings of Thomas Helwys*. Edited by Joseph Early. Macon, GA: Mercer University Press, 2009.

Henry, Matthew. *Matthew Henry's Commentary on the Whole Bible*. Iowa Falls, IA: World Bible Publishers, n.d.

Keller, Tim. *The Prodigal God: Recovering the Heart of the Christian Faith*. New York: Dutton, 2008.

Kendall, R. T. *Calvin and English Calvinism to 1649*. London: Oxford University Press, 1979.

Kevan, Ernest. *The Grace of Law: A Study in Purian Theology*. Ligonier, PA: Soli Deo Gloria, 1993.

Lane, Anthony. Review of *Calvin and English Calvinism to 1649*, by R. T. Kendall. *Themelios* 6 (1980) 29–31.

Lloyd-Jones, Martyn. *Studies in the Sermon on the Mount*. Vol. 1–2. Grand Rapids: Eerdmans, 1962.

Lovelace, R. C. "The Anatomy of Puritan Piety: English Puritan Devotional Literature, 1600–1640." In *Christian Spirituality III*, edited by L. Dupré and D. E. Saliers, 294–323. New York: Crossroad, 1989.

Manton, Thomas. *The Works of Thomas Manton*. 22 vols. Birmingham, AL: Solid Ground, 2008.

Milton, Michael. "The Pastoral Predicament of Vavasor Powell (1617–1670): Eschatological Fervor and Its Relationship to the Pastoral Ministry." *Journal of Evangelical Theological Society* 43/3 (Sept 2000) 517–27.

Ortlund, Dane. "Justified by Faith, Judged According to Works: Another Look at the Pauline Paradox." *Journal of the Evangelical Theological Society* 52/2 (June 2009) 323–39.

Owen, John. *An Exposition of Hebrews.* London: Johnstone and Hunter, 1855.

———. *The Works of John Owen.* Vol. 1–16. Edited by W. H. Goold. 1850. Reprint, Edinburgh: Banner of Truth, 1977.

Packer, J. I. *A Quest for Godliness: The Puritan Vision of the Christian Life.* Wheaton, IL: Crossway, 1990.

Pearse, Edward. *The Best Match; or, The Soul's Espousal to Christ.* Morgan, PA: Soli Deo Gloria, 1994.

Perkins, William. *A Godly and Learned Exposition Upon Christ's Sermon on the Mount.* In *The Works of William Perkins.* London: John Legatt, 1631.

———. *A Treatise Tending unto a Declaration, Whether a Man Be in the Estate of Damnation, or In the Estate of Grace.* In *The Works of William Perkins.* London: John Legatt, 1608.

———. *The Whole Treatise of the Cases of Conscience: Distinguished into Three Parts.* London: John Legatt, 1632.

Piper, John. *The Future of Justification: A Response to N. T. Wright.* Wheaton, IL: Crossway, 2007.

Powell, Vavasor. *Saving Faith Discovered in Three Heavenly Conferences.* In *A Guide to Eternal Glory; or, Brief Directions to All Christians How to Attain Everlasting Salvation; To Which are Added Several Other Excellent Divine Tracts.* London, 1699.

———. *The Scripture's Concord.* London, 1646.

Reid, W. Stanford. Review of *Calvin and English Calvinism to 1649,* by R. T. Kendall. *Westminster Theological Journal* 43 (1980) 155–64.

Schreiner, Tom. *The Law and Its Fulfillment: A Pauline Theology of Law.* Grand Rapids: Baker, 2001.

Sibbes, Richard. *The Bruised Reed.* 1630. Reprint, Edinburgh: Banner of Truth, 1998.

Stott, John. *Between Two Worlds: The Challenge of Preaching Today.* Grand Rapids: Eerdmans, 1982.

Swinnock, George. *The Works of George Swinnock.* 1868. Reprint, Edinburgh: Banner of Truth, 1992.

Venning, Ralph. *The Sinfulness of Sin; or, The Plague of Plagues.* 1669. Reprint, Edinburgh: Banner of Truth, 1965.

Watson, Thomas. *The Beatitudes: An Exposition of Matthew 5:1–12.* 1660. Reprint, Edinburgh: Banner of Truth, 1994.

———. *A Body of Divinity Contained in Sermons Upon the Westminster's Catechism.* 1890. Reprint, London: Banner of Truth, 1958.

White, James. *The God Who Justifies: The Doctrine of Justification.* Minneapolis: Bethany House, 2001.

Wilcox, Thomas. *A Guide to Eternal Glory; or, Brief Directions to All Christians, How to Attain a True and Saving Interest in Christ, In Order to Their Everlasting Salvation.* London, 1676.

Williams, Roger. *The Complete Writings of Roger Williams.* 7 vols. 1867. Reprint, Iron Oaks, AR: Baptist Standard Bearer, 1963.

Wright, N. T. *What Saint Paul Really Said: Was Saul of Tarsus the Real Founder of Christianity?* Grand Rapids: Eerdmans, 1997.

Yuille, J. Stephen *Puritan Spirituality: The Fear of God in the Affective Theology of George Swinnock.* Milton Keynes, UK: Paternoster, 2008.

———. *The Inner Sanctum of Puritan Piety: John Flavel's Doctrine of Mystical Union with Christ.* Grand Rapids: Reformation Heritage, 2007.

www.ingramcontent.com/pod-product-compliance
Lightning Source LLC
Chambersburg PA
CBHW070920180426

43192CB00038B/2098